Legendary
Service

Legendary Service

The Key Is to Care

Ken Blanchard

Kathy Cuff & Vicki Halsey

NEW YORK   CHICAGO   SAN FRANCISCO

ATHENS   LONDON   MADRID

MEXICO CITY   MILAN   NEW DELHI

SINGAPORE   SYDNEY   TORONTO

5 6 7 8 9 0   DOC/DOC   1 2 0 9 8 7 6 5

ISBN 978-0-07-181904-6
MHID   0-07-181904-5

e-ISBN 978-0-07-181785-1
e-MHID   0-07-181785-9

Book design by Lee Fukui and Mauna Eichner

Library of Congress Cataloging-in-Publication Data

Blanchard, Kenneth H.
  Legendary service : the key is to C.A.R.E. / Ken Blanchard, Victoria Halsey, and Kathy Cuff.
    pages cm
  ISBN 978-0-07-181904-6 (hardback) — ISBN 0-07-181904-5 (hardback)
  1. Customer services. 2. Customer services—Management. 3. Customer relations. I. Halsey, Victoria. II. Cuff, Kathy. III. Title.
  HF5415.5.B527 2014
  658.8'12—dc23
                                                              2014007861

McGraw-Hill Education books are available at special quantity discounts to use as premiums and sales promotions or for use in corporate training programs. To contact a representative, please visit the Contact Us pages at www.mhprofessional.com.

*Dedicated to all who believe
legendary customer service is the
critical link to making any
organization successful*

Contents

Contents

Introduction

When we were creating the Legendary Service® customer service training program for The Ken Blanchard Companies®, we asked people in organizations two questions:

1. *Why is customer service important?*

2. *What do you want your customers to know?*

And we always got the same answers:

1. *If customers are happy, they'll come back, and we'll be successful.*

2. *We want our customers to know we care about them so that they'll keep coming back.*

As a customer, why do *you* return again and again to a favorite store or business? It's not just about product quality.

Research shows customers return because of the way the people make them *feel.*

Sounds simple enough—let your customers know you care.

So, if demonstrating care for customers is so important and so simple, why isn't every organization doing it? After all, we all know it's far more cost-effective to keep the customers you have than to recruit new customers continuously to replace them.

Turn the page and meet Kelsey Young, a determined, optimistic young woman who is finishing her business degree while working part-time at Ferguson's, a discount store chain where happy customers are in short supply. Kelsey learns through her Legendary Service course at a local university that caring for customers is a fundamental part of business success. Longing to prove she has a future with Ferguson's and can help the company face the threat of an intimidating competitor, Kelsey works with her department manager to change things for the better. Through some surprising turns, Kelsey discovers how Legendary Service, or the lack of it, can shape an organization's future in a significant way—and how one person really *can* make a difference.

Now more than ever, it's time for people in organizations to learn to care for their customers. And you will, by reading this book and applying the ICARE model—the same model we've trained to top clients for years. Customer-facing employees will learn that no matter what level they are in the organization, they have the power to create a loyal, returning customer with each and every interaction. And leaders will discover how creating a Culture of Service begins with practicing a service mindset with their people so they will care for customers in a way that can significantly impact the organization's bottom line. Whether a CEO or a part-time employee like Kelsey, every person can make a difference—and customer service, both internal and external, is *everyone's* job.

I'm thrilled to have worked on this book with Kathy Cuff and Vicki Halsey, who are coauthors of our Legendary Service customer service training program and two of our company's top trainers and consultants. Kathy and Vicki have spent years teaching clients from every industry that even when you have a great product, you're only as successful as your customer service—and that Legendary Service creates loyal customers who come back for more.

When all is said and done, it really *is* simple—the key is to *care*. So put your feet up, enjoy the story, and let us show you how.

—Ken Blanchard
coauthor of
The One Minute Manager®

Legendary Service

1

A Frustrating Transaction

"**I need to return this** coffeemaker I bought a few weeks ago," the customer said, handing the sales associate the appliance in an open box.

"May I ask the reason for the return?" asked the young associate.

"Yes—the coffee doesn't come out as hot as I'd like it. I've already bought a different brand at another store, and I need a refund or a credit. I can't find the receipt."

"Not a problem," said the salesperson with a smile. "I just need to get a signature from the manager on duty and I'll be right back." She turned and headed toward the service desk.

The manager frowned as the young woman approached him and placed the coffeemaker box on the counter.

"We can't take this back, Kelsey," he said as he lifted the top flap and glanced inside. "It's been used. Is there a receipt?"

"No."

"Then it's a definite no. We have no idea how long the customer has had it."

Kelsey protested. "But wait—last week, Laurie told me small appliances could always be returned for store credit, no matter what, if the customer wasn't satisfied."

"Not without a receipt," said the manager. "I'm surprised Laurie told you that—she's been at this desk longer than I have." He pushed the box toward Kelsey. "Just tell the customer it's store policy—we can't take back used appliances without a receipt."

When Kelsey explained to the customer what the manager on duty had said, the woman glared at her with annoyance.

"How could I know what kind of coffee this made without opening it and using it? And every other place gives store credit when I don't have a receipt. Your policies don't make sense." She picked up the box and began to turn away, then looked back at Kelsey. "And you said there wouldn't be a problem."

"I'm so sorry," said Kelsey. She felt like such a jerk as she watched the woman walk away. That customer wasn't coming back—and Kelsey didn't blame her.

2

An Intriguing
Course

On the first day of the summer quarter, Kelsey Young sat down to begin her final college course. She was curious to know how the professor was going to spend eight weeks talking about customer service. Just then, the friendly-looking man at the front table who had been fidgeting with the cord on his laptop looked up and began to speak.

"Hello, everyone. I'm Professor Hartley, and I want to welcome you all to my course on Legendary Service. As business students, you need to know right up front that this is not only going to be the best course you've ever taken, but also one of the most important."

The professor chuckled. Kelsey could tell he didn't take himself too seriously.

"I know that sounds arrogant. Let me explain what I mean. You may think it's kind of odd to have a college course about customer service. But I want you to think about this: When was the last time you were on the receiving end of *great* customer service? Not just okay or pretty good service—*really excellent* service. When was the last time you wanted to tell other people about a fantastic customer service experience you had?"

The room was silent. A few students looked around to see if anyone was going to respond.

"You're having a little difficulty remembering that far back, aren't you? Aha! Maybe Legendary Service isn't as easy to come by as you thought. I'm convinced most managers tell their frontline people to be friendly and give great service, but they don't explain how to deliver it. You're actually going to learn how to do it.

"There aren't a lot of courses like this one—in fact, it took me quite a while to convince our curriculum people to include it in the business degree program. But I think it's wrong to have a major in management that doesn't include a core course in customer service. Why do I say this? Because when it comes to being successful in business, everything boils down to relationships. And relationships are built through service. Companies that see the importance of building relationships with their people and their customers are the ones that succeed in the long run. Business curriculum focuses mainly on the head, not the heart—and I think that's a mistake."

Professor Hartley turned to the projection screen at the front of the room and said, "All right, are you ready for the first major point of this course?" He tapped a key on his laptop and a quotation filled the screen:

> Customer loyalty is what you get
> when you create a motivating
> environment for your people.

"Great companies realize their most important customers are their own people—employees and managers. If leaders take care of their people and encourage them to bring their brains to work, the people will go out of their way to take care of the customers. When that happens, the customers will want to come back, which will ensure that the company is profitable."

Kelsey wasn't convinced. *How can it be that simple?* she thought. *Professor Hartley obviously hasn't shopped where I work. The managers there don't take care of their people or their customers!* She thought about her interaction with the angry customer who had tried to return the coffeemaker and frowned as she recalled her own frustration at having been put in such an awkward position.

"How many of you are currently employed, either part-time or full-time?" the professor asked.

Most of the students raised their hands.

"Keep your hands up and let me ask you a follow-up question." He paused for effect.

"How many of you *hate* your job?"

Kelsey lowered her hand but was stunned to see that almost all of the hands stayed in the air.

"Okay, here's a new question: Does anyone here actually *love* their job?"

All of the hands went down and only three others came up. Kelsey's certainly was not one of them. She guessed that most days, her opinion of her job was about halfway between love and hate.

Professor Hartley got serious. "This course is very hands-on. As we go along, I want you to take what you learn about Legendary Service and put it into practice, in whatever way you can, to create a better workplace for yourself and for the people around you. Regardless of how the place is run, or whether or not you're a manager, *you* can make a difference for your coworkers and your customers by showing you care about them and really want to serve them.

"Your first assignment is all about building relationships. It requires you to focus on three things this week at work. These three little ideas can change the way your customers feel about you, because you are going to give them a personal service experience."

The professor tapped his laptop and three numbered points appeared on the screen:

1. Learn and use the customer's name.
2. Talk about something other than the transaction.
3. Be friendly.

"First, learn the customer's name and use it as often as you can. People love to hear their names. Second, talk about something that's *not* related to your transaction. Admire the customer's watch or their shoes, ask them about their day so far, or talk about the weather. And the third thing is very simple, but increasingly rare: *just be friendly*, people! If you're face-to-face, look the person in the eye and give them a sincere smile. If you're serving your customer on the phone or online, make sure your interaction with them is positive and pleasant.

"I know everyone here can do all these things without much trouble—but I want you to deliberately focus on doing them, at least at first, to make them a habit. For those of you who aren't employed right now, remember that it goes both ways. If you use these tips now when you have interactions with service providers, the process will come naturally when you go back to work and interact with your customers. At the end of the week, write a two-page paper that gives some real specifics about what happened when you carried out these three ideas.

"I think you're in for a surprise. Because when you put your customers first, believe it or not, you're going to notice an immediate difference in how *you* feel about your job. Remember—relationships make the difference."

He makes it sound so easy, thought Kelsey as she gathered her materials and left class. She was unsure about whether the professor's methods would work at Ferguson's, the large discount store chain where she worked. Most of the time, the store was short-staffed, so spending extra time with customers would take her away from her other tasks. Making a real difference there would be an uphill battle.

As she drove to the gym that afternoon, Kelsey continued to think about what she'd learned. She knew the managers at Ferguson's could benefit from the knowledge and suggestions Professor Hartley had shared. There was plenty of room for improvement in how they treated the employees and customers, and it bothered her. Unfortunately, experiences like the one with the customer and the coffeemaker weren't unusual at Ferguson's. In the year Kelsey had been working in the Home and Office Department, she had gone home aggravated many nights, wishing she could work somewhere else. But as an undergraduate student finishing her degree, working part-time, and living with her grandmother in order to pay for college, she felt stuck. She knew finding another job that offered both health benefits and hours that worked with her school schedule would be next to impossible.

Happily, at the end of this course, Kelsey would finally earn her business degree. Listening to Professor Hartley made her hopeful that the lessons she would learn about service would help her progress in the career she'd set her sights on—retail management. She was on track to move to full-time status with Ferguson's, which was the next step toward an entry-level manager role. Even if she didn't stay with the company, Kelsey knew she was getting experience and building her résumé. She had made several friends at the store and had plenty of good days to balance the bad ones. Her ultimate goal was to own her own shop one day—and to be the kind of leader people would trust, respect, and want to work with. That thought kept her going—even though she knew that day was a long way off.

Kelsey hurried through Ferguson's parking lot on her way to the weekly Monday morning Home and Office Department meeting. She noticed a customer trying to load grocery bags into her SUV while simultaneously putting her screaming twins into their car seats. Because Kelsey was already running late, she felt herself hesitate for a split second before she stopped to help.

"Hi, my name's Kelsey, and I work here at Ferguson's," she said to the woman over the wailing of the toddlers. "Looks like you could use some help—let me load your groceries in the back so that you can have your hands free." She got right to work without waiting for an answer.

"Thanks a lot," said the harried mother as she turned her attention to her twins.

Kelsey thought about the three things the professor had said to try. It didn't seem like the right situation to ask the customer's name, but she decided to make small talk while loading the car.

"You're out nice and early getting your shopping done. I guess that's one way to beat the crowds."

The woman chuckled at Kelsey's statement as she finished with her toddlers. "We've been up for three hours already. But there was only one register open just now and a long line of customers waiting, so it took quite a while—and now the boys are overdue for their nap."

"I'm sorry—that must have been frustrating. Is there anything else I can do?" Kelsey asked.

"No, but thanks for stopping to help—you've renewed my faith in this store." The customer got into the driver's seat.

"I hope you have a great day!" said Kelsey as she waved and began to jog toward the store with the empty cart.

Kelsey was glad she'd stopped to help—especially when the woman mentioned her irritation at the long checkout line. She told herself being late for the meeting was a worthwhile trade-off for turning around a disgruntled customer. It's all about relationships, right?

Kelsey knew her department manager, Steven Walker, would say something when she walked into the meeting room. He was a stickler for punctuality. But she also knew he was a good manager with good intentions. He always arranged her work shifts around her school schedule, and he worked such long hours at the store that it almost seemed as if he lived there.

Just as Kelsey had predicted, Steven said, "Nice of you to join us, Kelsey," as she entered the meeting room as quietly as she could.

"I'm sorry." She'd explain her tardiness to him later.

After going through the weekly sales numbers and staff schedule, Steven looked up from his papers. "As you all know, ShopSmart is opening a store right down the road in a few months. A lot of Ferguson's customers are going to be attracted to that store, so we need to come up with some great ideas for how we can keep our customers—and their money—here at Ferguson's. Senior management is hinting that if we don't figure out something soon, a lot of us could be looking for work. I really need to hear your thoughts. Does anyone have any suggestions on what we can start doing, *today*, to serve our customers better?"

When Kelsey could see that no one was responding, she raised her hand. "I just started a customer service course at State, and our professor talked about how the customer needs to come first—it creates customer loyalty. In fact, that's why I was late—because I stopped in the parking lot to help a customer who was trying to load bags into her car while her two kids were crying."

"That's a pretty good reason for being late—I'll give you a pass this time," Steven said with a smirk. "Did your professor say anything else?"

"Yes, he told us about three ways we can give customers a personal experience. He said these three things can make a big difference in the way our customers feel about us."

"That's good—three things. Let's hear what they are." Steven seemed interested.

"The first one is to try to learn the name of your customer and use it when you're talking to them. People like the sound of their names. The second one, um—" She blanked for a moment. "Oh—talk about something that doesn't have anything to do with your sale, like maybe the customer's kids or the upcoming weekend, to show you're interested in them as people. And the third one is just to be nice and smile. Have a friendly face."

"I like it!" Steven said enthusiastically as he clapped his hands together. "Everyone, this is simple stuff—find out your customer's name and use it while you're helping them; talk about something besides the sale—try to build a little connection; and then just smile and stay focused on them. I know all of you can do these things today, right? Better yet, see if you can keep it up all week long!" A few heads nodded in agreement. With that, Steven dismissed the group to start their day on the sales floor.

Kelsey felt encouraged by Steven's willingness to use her suggestions. Ever since the buzz about ShopSmart had started, Kelsey had been hearing people at work talk about applying there. She hoped Steven's positive call to action this morning would help to change their minds. Rather than thinking about quitting, maybe everyone would start thinking about ways to keep the store's customers and create a happier work environment right here at Ferguson's.

Kelsey attached her name tag to her shirt and headed from the break room into the store. *Professor Hartley wants us to apply the concepts we're learning to our jobs,* she thought. *It worked once this morning already, so I guess I'll try it all day today and see if it makes a difference like he said it would.*

Walking up the aisle, she noticed a woman standing in front of a back-to-school display, staring down at a piece of paper in her hand. As Kelsey approached her, she could see it was a list with the words *Brendan's Dorm Room* scribbled at the top.

"May I help you find something?" Kelsey asked the customer.

"Oh, yes," the woman said with an anxious laugh as she looked up from the paper. "My son is going off to college, and he needs just about everything. He's been busy working this summer, so I told him I would do this for him." She shook her head. "I can't believe it's almost time for him to go."

Kelsey gave the woman a sympathetic smile. "I know my mom was sad when I moved here to go to college and live with my grandma. But if you're like my mom, you're happy your son is continuing his education."

"Oh, believe me, I don't want him watching TV on my couch forever—I just hate the thought of him going so far away. Actually, I'd really love some help with this list, if you don't mind."

"Sure—I'm happy to help. My name's Kelsey." Kelsey threw it out there, hoping the customer would say her name in return.

"I'm Diane," said the customer with a smile.

Kelsey and her customer, Diane, walked all through the store and filled a shopping cart with bedding, school supplies, computer accessories—even a small microwave. After they had all the items on the list and a few extra things, Kelsey had one last suggestion.

"Right now, lots of people are buying a book we carry about how to succeed in college. It has some good basic tips on studying and time management. It might be a nice gift for you to give your son to show your support."

"That's a great idea," said Diane. "I know he's a little nervous about whether he can handle college work. Not that he admits that to me, of course," she said with a laugh.

"Don't worry, he's going to be missing you soon enough and wishing for a home-cooked meal!" Kelsey said. Diane laughed again as Kelsey hurried to the book department, grabbed a copy of the book, and brought it back to Diane.

"Thank you, Kelsey—I never would've thought of this," Diane said as Kelsey handed her the book. "I really appreciate your taking the time to help me find everything so that I can set Brendan up for success." She paused. "You know, I'm not used to this level of service from Ferguson's. You really took the time to help me and actually cared about what I needed."

"I'm glad I could help, Diane," said Kelsey with a smile. Diane reached out and shook her hand.

That interaction went so well, Kelsey decided to try the same personal, caring approach with other customers. She even kept track—and she ended the day with a total of six customers specifically commenting on her service or thanking her for her help. The most surprising thing for Kelsey was how good *she* felt about these interactions—just as the professor had predicted. In fact, it ended up being one of the best days she'd ever had at work.

3

What Is Legendary Service?

As she searched for a parking space at school the next morning, Kelsey thought about the challenge Steven had given the department staff concerning finding ways to beat the competition. She also thought about what Professor Hartley had said in the first class: if a company takes care of its people, the people will take care of the customers, and the customers will want to come back. Once again, she wondered: *Could it really be that simple?*

Later, when the professor was speaking to the class, it was as if he'd read her mind.

"What's the difference between a great company and a mediocre company?" asked Professor Hartley.

Getting no response, he said, "Okay, I'll tell you. Great companies have learned how to let their customers know that they care about them and want to earn their business. They also know the importance of building relationships with both *internal* customers—their people—and *external* customers— the ones who buy their product or service. Focusing on relationships, such as applying the three points I asked you to write about in your papers, is an organization's most powerful competitive advantage. Let's do a quick survey to demonstrate this."

On the whiteboard, the professor drew a box and inside it wrote the numbers 1 through 10.

1	2	3	4	5	6	7	8	9	10

"I want you to think about all the activities you're involved in, things you do, and places you go in a given week— shopping in stores; shopping online; upgrading your phone; or going to a movie, to a restaurant, or to the dry cleaner. Now think about the kind of service you get at each of those places. If you had to average out the service you receive, where would it fall on this chart? The number 1 represents service that's so bad it couldn't get any worse, and 10 means you get treated like a rock star. When you know your number, come up and make a check mark on the board next to the number you're thinking of."

When all the class members were back in their seats, he said to them, "Now look at the board and tell me the rough average of everyone's check marks."

"Five," several students called out.

"And what kind of score would you call that?" asked the professor.

"Average."

"Well, I don't know about you, but I don't brag about anything that's average. Do any of you?" he asked.

The students shook their heads; some chuckled under their breath, and a few said, "No."

"Now think about your workplace. If your customers rated the type of service they typically receive, how would they rate it?"

Again, a number of students called out, "Five." The only exception Kelsey heard was one of the people who had said she loved her job, and she called out, "Nine."

"Even though most of you rated your place of employment as delivering average service to its customers, I doubt that the CEO of any organization that wanted to stay in business would be okay with that score. In fact, most companies would probably say they'd like to be *legendary* in the eyes of their customers. That would be like scoring a 10 on our scale.

"Let's look at how we define *Legendary Service*." Professor Hartley tapped a key on his laptop, and the screen read:

> **Legendary Service:**
> Consistently delivering ideal service
> that keeps customers coming back
> and results in a competitive edge
> for your organization.

"Simply put, companies can achieve Legendary Service by showing their customers they *care* about them."

Kelsey smiled as she thought about the interaction she'd had with Diane, the mom who was sending her son off to college. Diane had said she could tell that Kelsey really *cared*.

"Your next assignment is to create a five-minute presentation for the class where you give examples from places where you shop, visit, and work—in person, on the phone, or online—where people are showing they care about you or others," said the professor. "If you pay attention, you should be able to find plenty of material to fill up your time."

Kelsey could feel the gears turning in her brain. She felt she had a good start on the kind of attitude the professor was talking about. *Even though I've only been at Ferguson's for a year, I think I really might be able to help make a difference in the way the store does business.* Was this crazy? Could she help create a positive customer service culture at Ferguson's even though she wasn't a manager?

Kelsey decided not only to look for examples around her but also to try to create stories with her own customers.

If, with Steven's help, she could keep passing along Professor Hartley's concepts to her teammates at work, customers might begin to notice that Ferguson's service was improving. She actually found herself looking forward to going to work.

On her way home from class, Kelsey stopped at the pharmacy to pick up her grandma's blood pressure medicine. Kelsey had been going there for more than a year, but the jaded pharmacy clerk, Bianca, always acted as though she'd never seen her before in her life. Excited about the idea of creating great customer service even if *she* was the customer, Kelsey decided that today was the day she was going to win Bianca over.

As she approached the counter, she noticed a blue ribbon hanging below Bianca's name tag. It was embroidered with the word *WOW*.

"May I help you?" Bianca asked in a monotone as she stared at Kelsey, visibly bored.

"Hi, Bianca, good to see you again. How's your day going?" asked Kelsey with a smile.

"Fine," said Bianca, still expressionless.

Kelsey paused briefly and said, "Um, okay—do you have a prescription ready for Katherine Wilson?"

Bianca turned, pulled a small white bag out of the *W* basket, circled back to face Kelsey, and handed her the bag.

"That'll be four dollars."

Kelsey dug in her purse, pulled out a five-dollar bill, and, still smiling, handed it to Bianca. "I think it's so great my grandma can get her pills at a discount because she's on a fixed income," she said cheerfully, trying to make conversation. "By the way, what does your *WOW* ribbon stand for?"

Bianca looked down at the ribbon under her name tag. "Oh, that's to remind us to do things to make our customers say, 'Wow.'" She rolled her eyes and shook her head slightly.

Bianca tapped a few buttons on the register, exchanged bills, handed the change and the receipt to Kelsey, and said robotically, "Thank you for shopping with us. Come again." She immediately tilted her head to look at the customer standing behind Kelsey and droned, "Next."

Wow, thought Kelsey ironically.

It was obvious that instructing employees to "wow" customers or wear ribbons on their name tags wasn't enough to make great service magically happen. As Kelsey drove home, she realized that finding—or creating—the Legendary Service her professor had talked about might be trickier than she had anticipated.

As Kelsey walked up the steps to the front door of her grand-mother's house, she felt her mood lift, knowing that her grandma always had something cheerful to say when she walked in.

"Grandma Kate, I'm home," she called out, as she did every day.

No response. She knew her grandma should be home because she didn't drive and hadn't mentioned having plans with anyone.

"Grandma Kate?" Kelsey called a little louder as she started moving quickly from room to room. When she approached the kitchen, she could hear her grandma calling her name softly.

Kelsey turned the corner and saw her grandmother lying on the floor. She rushed over to her. "Oh, Grandma, are you okay?"

"Yes . . . yes, I'm okay," her grandmother said hesitantly. "It's nothing, really. A few minutes ago, I tripped on the rug in front of the sink and fell. And it's just like that commercial—I can't seem to pull myself back up. What a klutz!"

As Kelsey attempted to help her up, she could see that her grandma's left wrist was already bruised and swollen. Kelsey convinced her she needed to see a doctor, and they headed to the urgent care center.

The doctor on duty confirmed it was a moderate sprain, gave Kelsey a sheet of directions to follow at home for the first two to three days, and put Grandma Kate's wrist in a removable brace. "Keep the brace on as much as you can," he told Grandma Kate. "I'm referring you to the Move Right Physical

Therapy Clinic. Make an appointment there for early next week, once the swelling is down. They'll get you set up with some therapy." He turned to Kelsey and said, "I think you'll both really like this place. They're good at what they do and they really *care* about their patients."

Hmmm, Kelsey thought. *There's that word again!*

Back at home, Kelsey made Grandma Kate a cup of tea and helped her get comfortable in her chair before she called the physical therapy clinic. Because it was after five o'clock, she assumed it wouldn't be open, but she wanted to leave a message.

"Good evening, and thanks for calling Move Right Clinic," a friendly voice answered after the second ring. "This is Barbara; how may I help you?"

"Oh! I didn't expect anyone to answer. I need to schedule an appointment for my grandmother. She sprained her wrist today," explained Kelsey.

"I'm sorry to hear that. I'll be happy to help you," said Barbara. "Yes, we're open until seven o'clock three nights a week to accommodate our customers' work schedules. Let's see what time we have available that would work best for your grandmother."

After getting all the information she needed, Barbara scheduled Grandma Kate to come in late Monday afternoon. "That should allow time for the swelling on her wrist to subside before we start working with her. Have her keep it in the brace the doctor gave her, and I'll see you both on Monday," she said.

"Thanks so much." Kelsey hung up the phone and turned to Grandma Kate with a smile. "She was so sweet. I think we *will* both like this place, Grandma."

The next morning at work, Kelsey overheard two of her teammates talking while they stocked the shelves.

Amy grumbled, "It's taking us three times as long as it should to fill the shelves because the customers keep asking us questions. Nobody takes the time to look for things on their own."

"I know what you mean," Rob said. "The other day Steven practically accused me of going slow on purpose, but it was because I had to keep stopping to help customers. I couldn't get anything done."

Kelsey approached the two and said in a hushed tone, "Guys, don't forget—we have to keep showing our customers we care about them so that we don't lose them to ShopSmart."

Rob looked at Kelsey. "Ha! It's not like the managers here treat *me* like *they* care. I work hard, and I do everything they ask me to do, but do I ever hear, 'Thanks, Rob,' or, 'You're doing a great job, Rob'? No. I feel like I'm just a number around here. Why should I go out of my way to act like *I* care?"

Amy nodded in agreement. "I hear ShopSmart pays the same and treats their people better. I'm thinking of going for a job over there."

Kelsey had to admit that Rob and Amy had a point. Senior managers at Ferguson's didn't do anything to show the employees they cared about them. It made her think about what Professor Hartley had said about internal customers: *focusing on relationships with both external and internal customers is an organization's most powerful competitive advantage.* Ferguson's managers had a lot of work to do if they were going to win over not only their external customers but also their internal customers—their employees—and keep them from leaving.

Grandma Kate was standing in the living room, purse in hand, when Kelsey got home from work that afternoon.

"Hi, Grandma—what's going on?" asked Kelsey, amused at the mischievous expression on her grandmother's face.

"You've been working too hard, Kelsey. I want you to turn around right now, and I'm going to treat you to dinner. I've made reservations at Giuseppe's, your favorite place."

"Grandma, you don't have to do that," Kelsey softly protested.

"You know I love to surprise you—and you're always doing things for me," said Grandma Kate. "Besides, I need to get out of the house—this sprained wrist is making me feel like an invalid. I need a distraction. Of course, you'll have to do the driving."

"Okay, then, if you insist!" Kelsey laughed, turned around, and marched out the front door, with Grandma Kate close behind.

As Kelsey and Grandma Kate entered the tiny Italian restaurant a few minutes later, the scent of garlic and marinara was so intense, they could almost see it.

"Mrs. Wilson! Kelsey! How wonderful to see you again. It's been too long," said the owner, a dark-haired man standing at the host station. He grabbed two menus and, with a sweep of his arm, invited them to follow him. "I'll seat you at a window table—I remember, Mrs. Wilson, how you like to watch the people walk by."

"Ah, Giuseppe—I don't know how you can remember a little thing like that," said Grandma Kate, beaming.

"Sometimes it's the little things that matter the most," Giuseppe answered with a smile. "Now let me tell you about tonight's specials. . . . "

All through dinner, the restaurant staff demonstrated to Kelsey and Grandma Kate what Legendary Service was all about. Not only had the owner himself greeted them by name and remembered their table preference, but the server was attentive and gracious, and the busser kept their water glasses and bread basket full. The food was excellent, as always, with portions that would supply leftovers for at least two days.

By the time the two women left the restaurant, the Friday night crowd was in full swing, with a line of people stretching down the sidewalk. Kelsey remembered Giuseppe once saying he had thought about expanding the size of the restaurant or opening another location, but he didn't want to risk losing the family atmosphere or the reputation for service that he had built over the years.

Kelsey was convinced, now more than ever, that great customer service was the key to a successful business.

4

A Catalyst
for Change

Steven started off the next Monday morning department meeting with a personal observation.

"This past week, our store manager received a letter from a customer praising someone in our department for their service," he began. "I read the letter more than once and thought about how good it made me feel—and how proud. And I started realizing that as your department manager, I'm in a position to be able to create that same sense of pride in you all. I don't think I've been doing a very good job of that."

Kelsey was impressed. Steven didn't usually show his vulnerable side.

"I've asked you to start focusing more on our customers and working to build rapport with them, and that's still our main objective. But we also need to remember to serve each other when we can, and to treat each other in the same positive way we treat our customers. I'm no different from you in this area. So I'm going to make a point of being more mindful about noticing the good things that are happening around our department—when shelves are well stocked and aisles are clean, or when I see you helping each other or taking extra care with a customer. In other words, I'm going to work on catching you doing things right. You all deserve the same care and focus as our customers."

Kelsey's teammates seemed to be encouraged by what Steven was saying. A few of them whispered to each other and a few smiled as Steven continued.

"Our department numbers have been looking very good over the past couple of weeks—even better than last year at this time, which is excellent. With the Back to School campaign going on, Home and Office is one of the busiest departments in the store. I know you've all been working hard to keep the merchandise stocked and to help customers find what they need, and I think you're doing a great job with that. We haven't had any customer complaints for quite a while, and we've even received some compliments. As a matter of fact, I want to share the letter I mentioned earlier. It's about your teammate, Kelsey Young."

Kelsey couldn't hide her surprise as Steven began reading the letter out loud:

Dear Store Manager,

I was in Ferguson's recently to buy some things for my son, who is going away to college. I wanted to let you know how one of your salespeople, Kelsey, helped me find what I needed—and, even more important, how she made me feel.

I was a bit emotional since my son will be going away soon, and Kelsey was able to empathize with me. She turned my shopping trip from something I was dreading into a fun and enjoyable experience. She not only helped me find everything on my list, but she also gave me great ideas for other things he would need that I hadn't thought of. She was kind and patient with me and seemed to care about my situation.

I just thought you would like to know what a great representative you have in Kelsey. I haven't always received this kind of service at Ferguson's, but I will definitely be back to your store and will share this experience with my friends.

Sincerely,
Diane Hernandez

"Great job, Kelsey," said Steven. "Thanks for representing our department, and our store, so well."

Although Kelsey was thoroughly embarrassed by Steven's reading the letter to everyone, she also felt proud. Maybe if her coworkers thought that they, too, might get some kind of recognition, it would motivate them to take the initiative and help customers.

"Okay now, let's get down to business." Steven clapped his hands together. "Who has some great ideas for how we can team up and beat the competition?"

Everyone looked around to see if someone else was going to say something. Aside from a few quiet snickers and murmured comments, the room was filled with a long and awkward silence.

"Really? Nobody?" said Steven, visibly disappointed. "I thought you'd all jump at the chance to pummel those other guys. Where's your fighting spirit?" He attempted a smile but again got no response from the group.

Kelsey wanted to raise her hand to share an idea, but she knew she would look like a goody-goody after that letter. She remained silent with the rest of the group.

"Okay, let's get to work—and remember, everybody, the customer comes first," Steven said with a wave of his hand. The room cleared out quickly, but Kelsey stayed behind. She felt sorry for her boss. She could tell he was trying.

"Thanks for sharing that letter, Steven. Do you think I could make a copy of it? I know my grandma would love to read it."

"Sure," he said, smiling as he handed her the letter. "Just be sure I get the original back so that I can put it in your file."

Since Steven still seemed to be receptive, Kelsey decided to share her idea from a few minutes earlier. "Do you remember last week when I mentioned the customer service course

I'm taking? It's part of my business degree, and it's all about the importance of building relationships with both internal and external customers by showing them you care about them."

"That's right. You shared some good ideas with us," said Steven, interested. "If that letter's any indication, you must be coming to work and practicing what you're learning."

"That's exactly what I'm doing—and I'm realizing it's kind of fun to try to impress customers. It's actually helping me enjoy my job a lot more. For instance, it might sound corny, but I've set a goal for today of getting a smile out of every customer I talk to."

Steven looked surprised. "Terrific. It's a win-win, then." They both laughed. Steven's mood seemed brighter. "I really like this new enthusiasm you have about service. Maybe you can help me create that same energy in the rest of the team. Why don't you keep me in the loop on the things you're learning, and we can try to spread your positive outlook to the whole department. We could be a kind of learning lab for the whole store. I know we need to do something soon if we're going to compete with ShopSmart. "

They agreed to meet each week for a few minutes before the Monday morning meeting. Kelsey would update Steven on what she had learned, and he could pass it along to the team if he felt it was relevant.

For the first time since she started at Ferguson's, Kelsey left work that day with the feeling that she was part of something important—and that she had taken the first step toward positive change.

"Grandma Kate, I'm home! Time for your physical therapy appointment," called Kelsey as she stepped into the house.

Grandma Kate laughed as she came down the hall, carrying her purse. "You know me, honey—I've been ready for an hour."

As they drove to the clinic, Kelsey shared how her boss had read the customer's letter to everyone at the meeting.

"I'm glad you made a copy. I can't wait to read it," said Grandma Kate. "You know, honey, when you speak from your heart and treat people with kindness, it always comes back to you. It's wonderful that you feel helping others is part of your job. That attitude is going to serve you well wherever your life takes you."

Grandma Kate was always sharing words of wisdom, but Kelsey found it very interesting that this time it was essentially the same message she'd been hearing from her professor about service—to have a caring attitude toward others.

"Good afternoon," said the smiling woman behind the counter as Kelsey and her grandmother walked into the clinic. The woman looked at Grandma Kate. "I'll bet you're Katherine Wilson."

"Yes, I am," said Grandma Kate. "I just go by Kate."

"I'll make a note of that. My name is Barbara. If you wouldn't mind filling out these forms, I'll let Iris know you're here." She handed Grandma Kate a clipboard and a pencil.

Grandma Kate took the paperwork, and she and Kelsey walked toward the chairs. They hadn't even had a chance to sit down when an inside door opened, and there stood a petite woman with a long black ponytail, wearing a white jacket and holding a folder.

"Mrs. Wilson?" she called as she looked directly at Grandma Kate, who waved her braced hand.

The woman smiled and walked over to them. "Don't bother sitting; you can come with me and fill out the papers in the exam room." She gently shook Grandma Kate's good hand and said warmly, "I'm Iris Wright, and I'll be working with you to get your wrist back up to speed." She turned to Kelsey and smiled.

"Hi. You must be Kelsey. You'll be bringing Mrs. Wilson to her appointments?" she asked as they shook hands. Kelsey nodded.

"Yes, she's my granddaughter and the sweetest driver in town," Grandma Kate answered for Kelsey. "Now—I've never been to a physical therapist before. Do I call you Dr. Wright?"

"Please, just call me Iris. I do have my doctoral degree in physical therapy, but I prefer to keep things more casual with my patients."

"All right, Iris—and you can call me Kate," said Grandma Kate with a smile.

"It's a deal. Now let's head back to the therapy room."

As they walked, Grandma Kate said, "Iris?"

"Yes, Kate?"

"I have a Tai Chi class that meets every Saturday in the park at the end of my street. I hope I won't have to give it up because of my sprain."

"I can't know for certain until I examine you, but you probably won't. Just tell your instructor about your injury and wear your brace, and I'm sure you'll be able to participate in most of the movements. It's very important for you to keep up with activities you enjoy, if at all possible. It's a key aspect of healing."

While examining Grandma Kate's wrist in the therapy room, Iris talked about her background as Kelsey finished filling out the forms. Iris shared that she had been the first in her family to graduate from college and that she owned the clinic, which had been in business for six years.

"As a matter of fact, while I'm talking about our team, let me introduce you to someone who will also be working with you." Iris opened the door slightly and called out, "Barbara, would you please ask Alex to come to Room 3 when he's available?"

A moment later, there was a knock on the door and a young man in a button-down shirt stepped into the room.

Iris said, "Mrs. Wilson and Kelsey, this is Alex, my physical therapy assistant and our office energizer. Alex, this is Mrs. Wilson and her granddaughter, Kelsey. Mrs. Wilson has a sprained wrist, so she'll be coming to see us for a while, and Kelsey will be coming with her."

"Great to meet you both," said Alex as he shook their hands enthusiastically. "Mrs. Wilson, Iris is the best—and when I work with you, I'll make things as easy for you as I can. We'll have you feeling like new in no time. Now if you'll excuse me, I've got to get to my next appointment." He said goodbye and left the room.

For the next half hour, Kelsey watched Iris take the time to thoroughly explain to Grandma Kate what she was doing as she worked on her wrist. Grandma Kate asked several questions and shared a few stories, but Iris didn't seem to mind and was patient and attentive. Kelsey was impressed at how happy and comfortable her grandmother seemed in this new environment.

At one point, when Grandma Kate was in the restroom, Iris said to Kelsey, "Your grandma is very sweet. It makes our jobs much easier when the patient has a positive attitude, and I know it will help her heal faster."

"My grandma is one of the most positive people I know, and you seem to be the same way. You obviously love what you do. In fact, everyone we've met here seems to love their job," said Kelsey.

"Yes, we really do. We have a great team here at the clinic—almost like a family. I'm fortunate to work with such caring and dedicated people. I know the customers can tell when the staff is happy."

Kelsey compared Iris's cheerful attitude about her workplace with that of her team at Ferguson's. *What a different mindset*, she thought.

"We'll need your grandmother to come to the clinic twice a week for probably four to six weeks to get her wrist back in shape," Iris said. "She'll be seeing either Alex or me."

"I'm sure she'll be happy to work with both of you," said Kelsey. "I'll have to fit her appointments into my schedule, but I don't think it will be a problem. I'm living with her while I work toward my business degree at State, so it's easy for me to drive her where she needs to go."

"That's great," Iris said with a smile. "I took a number of business courses at State while I was working toward my degree in physical therapy several years ago."

Grandma Kate came back into the room, took a deep breath, and said, "Okay, Kelsey, I'm ready when you are. I need to go home and soak these old bones in a nice hot bubble bath."

Iris laughed. "That sounds like my way to relax, Kate! I'm looking forward to your visits. I'll see you on Wednesday."

5

Ideal
Service

"**I really enjoyed your presentations**—you all did a great job," said Professor Hartley. "It's a good way to set up what we'll be focusing on for the rest of our course.

"Over the next several weeks, I'm going to introduce you to a model that uses the acronym ICARE. We'll take one letter from the model—one segment—at a time, and discuss it. You'll then go out into your world, find examples of that specific aspect of service—and also examples of where it's lacking—and write about your experiences. Now let's talk about service at a higher level."

He tapped his laptop and the ICARE model appeared on the screen with the first letter of the acronym identified.

I – **Ideal Service**

C –

A –

R –

E –

"Can anyone tell me if you think you've seen an example of *Ideal Service* since we were last together?" asked Professor Hartley.

His question was met with puzzled looks and low murmurs, but no one spoke up.

"Perhaps you need a bit more information on what I'm talking about. No matter what industry you're in, as a service provider you have the ability to demonstrate daily, through your actions, your words, and your behavior, that you believe service is important. Think of it as being in a Hall of Fame for serving others—people who provide Ideal Service are the best of the best. Here's our official definition of Ideal Service." He brought up the next slide.

Ideal Service:

Meeting the customer's needs on a
day-to-day basis by acting on the belief
that service is important.

As Kelsey listened to the professor and read the words on the slide, she found herself thinking about Iris and Barbara at the clinic.

"I want you to memorize this, so I'm going to leave it on the screen for a few minutes. Make a note of it," said the professor. "So—now that we're clear on the definition, which of you can think of a story you want to share about Ideal Service?"

A student named Nathan raised his hand.

"Last week my dad asked me if I'd do him a favor and take his car in because the warning light showed that he needed an oil change. I took it to the little auto shop in his neighborhood where he always goes. I gave the mechanic the keys, and while I was waiting, the owner of the place came into the waiting room to say hello. I asked him how business was, and he said, 'You know, a lot of my competitors are having a tough time in this economy, but our business is booming.'

"After I'd waited for about 15 minutes, the mechanic came in and told me the car didn't need an oil change after all. He said the service light isn't always accurate and the oil was probably good for at least another 2,000 miles. He had checked the engine for signs of wear and told me I was good to go. There was no charge! It blew me away. Now I know why my dad's been going back to the same place for 15 years and why that business is doing so well compared to its competitors."

As the other students were commenting to each other, Professor Hartley looked at Nathan and said brightly, "Thanks, Nathan. I think a few of us need to get the name and address of that place before you leave today." He turned to the class. "Notice what just happened here. That small act of goodwill may have cost that shop the price of one oil change—but it also may have generated five or six new customers just now, in this room, because Nathan told us that story. Does anyone else have an example of Ideal Service?"

Kelsey raised her hand and talked about how both Barbara and Iris from the Move Right clinic had shown they cared about their customers through the way they greeted Kelsey and her grandmother, took the time to explain procedures and answer questions, and made Grandma Kate feel comfortable and welcome.

When Kelsey had finished, Professor Hartley thanked her and said, "You don't have to be a genius to figure out that Ideal Service can make all the difference in whether or not a business is successful. So this week I want you to find one great example of Ideal Service and another that shows the *opposite* of Ideal Service. Write as much as you can about both situations—the person who provided the service, the organization they represented, and what they did to create a good or bad impression—and please remember to include *how it made you feel.*"

Kelsey hit the ground running when she got to Ferguson's later that day. She was determined to create her own examples of Ideal Service—and to do it in a way that would get a positive reaction from her customers.

Checking for misplaced items in the aisles, Kelsey walked around a corner and almost ran into a tall man who was bending to read a sign in front of the display of vacuum cleaners. Startled, he stood up and looked at Kelsey.

"Hey, I'm glad you're here," the man said when he realized Kelsey was an employee.

"So am I," she said with a smile. "I'm Kelsey."

"Uh . . . I'm Tom."

"Hi, Tom. What can I help you with?"

"I want to get my wife a vacuum cleaner for her birthday. She really deserves the best." He pointed to a display model. "This one looks pretty good, and it's on sale, too. What can you tell me about it?"

Kelsey's first thought was, *Oh, no—a vacuum cleaner is not a good birthday gift!* But she quickly realized her job was not to talk the customer out of a purchase—it was to provide Ideal Service.

"You're right—this model is very popular. It's the top-rated brand for performance. And, as I'll show you, the accessories are very easy to attach and take off." She demonstrated this by clicking one of the attachments onto the end of the hose and then removing it. "It's also one of the quieter models we sell."

"That would be a plus—I hate it when she's vacuuming while I'm trying to watch TV. The one we have now is really loud." Tom smiled at Kelsey.

She couldn't tell if he was kidding. *Ugh,* she thought. *He's more interested in his TV shows than in his wife. This is going to be a bigger challenge than I thought!*

"Is there anything else you'd like to know about this model?" she asked.

"I guess not—I think I'll take it," said Tom as he picked up the box next to the display. He paused. "You know, there *is* one more thing you might be able to help me with—even though you're kind of young."

That's great; now I'm too young. Tom's an interesting guy. This is turning into a perfect transaction, Kelsey thought sarcastically, trying not to grit her teeth as she smiled.

"I'll try my best, Tom—what else do you need?"

"Well—" Tom looked at the box he was holding. "Do you think my wife will like this? I mean, I know she'll like it because it's a really good one, but—" He looked at Kelsey. "If you were married and your husband gave this to you for your birthday, how would you react?"

Kelsey froze. *If I tell him what I really think, I'll lose this sale,* she thought. *Wait a minute—it's not about the sale, it's about giving him Ideal Service—which means meeting his needs because I believe service is important. Right now he needs an honest answer.*

"Since you asked me, Tom, I think if I were married and my husband gave me a vacuum cleaner for my birthday, even if it were the most amazing vacuum cleaner in the world, I'd be . . ." She searched for the right word. ". . . disappointed."

"I knew it!" exclaimed Tom as he broke into a toothy grin. "My brother told me it was a good idea, and I never agree with him on anything! I'm really glad you were honest with me." He put the box back on the shelf. Kelsey breathed a quiet sigh of relief mixed with mild concern at losing the sale—but she knew she'd done the right thing.

"Okay, Kelsey," said Tom as he rubbed his hands together. "Now let's take what I would've spent on the vacuum cleaner and use it to get my wife something she'll really like. I think if I work with you, I can figure this out. You seem to know what you're doing—and you seem to actually care about my wife having a happy birthday. What's better than that?"

Kelsey couldn't believe what had just happened—she'd pulled it off! Tom wasn't such a bad guy, after all. This experience was going to leave a lasting impression on him—and she'd still get a good sale for the store. Tom ended up choosing an elegant crystal vase, which he said he would fill with his wife's favorite flowers. Next, Kelsey accompanied him to the jewelry department, where her friend Rachel helped him pick out a beautiful bracelet.

Kelsey decided to write up this experience as part of her homework assignment. She was excited about writing a story in which she herself was in the role of the service provider who had delivered Ideal Service to her customer!

"Welcome back," Barbara greeted Grandma Kate and Kelsey as they walked into the clinic. Just then, Alex arrived in the waiting room as well.

"Hello, Mrs. Wilson. Hi, Kelsey. Nice to see you both again. How's the wrist feeling after your last session?"

"It's been a little sore, but I guess that goes with the territory," said Grandma Kate cheerfully.

"Well, come on back and let me take a look at it. Kelsey, would you like to come back as well, or wait out here?"

"Actually, I brought my laptop—I have to write a paper, so I'll just find a spot out here—but thanks," said Kelsey.

"We do have a reading room. It'll be nice and quiet for you to study there while I'm working with your grandma. It's just down that hall, the last door on the right." Alex gestured.

"That'll be perfect," said Kelsey with a smile. "No distractions." She walked to the reading room and was pleasantly surprised. It was small but nicely decorated and felt as comfortable as a living room.

By the time Grandma Kate's appointment was over, Kelsey had finished writing the Ideal Service story about her customer, Tom, and his near miss with the vacuum cleaner.

On the way home, Grandma Kate reiterated how nice everyone at the clinic was. "Alex treats me like I'm *his* grandmother."

Kelsey smiled, thankful that Alex, like Iris, was making her grandmother feel cared for—another example of the clinic's Ideal Service. Now she just needed a good example of service that was *not* ideal.

Because Kelsey didn't need to be at work until noon on Saturday, she had made a ten o'clock appointment for a haircut at a nice salon in town that she had been wanting to try.

When she walked in, she was impressed by the lofty ceilings and the elegant black-and-tan color scheme. Most of the stations were in use, and all of the stylists were fashionably dressed in black. Several people were sitting in the waiting area, reading magazines. Kelsey was looking forward to having her hair done at an upscale place like this. She walked up to the young man at the reception desk, who was staring down at an electronic tablet. When a minute had gone by and he hadn't acknowledged her, Kelsey cleared her throat softly.

The receptionist looked up and smiled. "Don't worry, I noticed you," he said.

"I have an appointment for ten o'clock with Bebe," said Kelsey, feeling slightly uncomfortable.

The receptionist turned back to the tablet, tapped it a few times, and said, "Oh, yes, are you Kelsey?" When she nodded, he said, "Okay, have a seat and Bebe will be with you as soon as she finishes with her client." He gestured toward a tall, thin stylist with brilliant red hair who was standing at the first station and taking a towel off the head of the customer sitting in front of her.

Kelsey sat down and picked up a magazine but kept an eye on Bebe. When Kelsey saw Bebe start to comb out the woman's wet hair and heard her say, "What kind of style are you looking for today?" she got up and walked back to the reception desk.

"Excuse me," Kelsey said. The receptionist looked up from his tablet. "My appointment was for ten o'clock, and now it's five after ten. I just heard Bebe ask her customer what kind of style she was looking for. Do you know how long she'll be?"

The receptionist looked at Kelsey and then looked over at Bebe. "Well, Bebe's a real perfectionist, so you never know with her."

Kelsey felt her cheeks getting red. "I'm sorry, but it doesn't seem right that I was on time for my appointment and it's pretty clear she's just started working with this customer."

"Oh, Bebe," the young man called over to the stylist, "would you please come over here for a second?" Bebe said something to her customer, then walked toward the desk, energetically chewing her gum.

The receptionist smiled at Bebe and pointed at Kelsey. "This customer would like to know how long it's going to take you to cut your client's hair."

Bebe laughed. "I have no idea!" she said loudly, snapping her gum. "Everybody's hair is different." She put her hand on her hip and looked at Kelsey. "Why do you need to know?"

"Because I'm your ten o'clock appointment," said Kelsey defensively. "It looks as if you started working with her just as I came in."

"Oh, yeah, she was pretty late, but she's a friend of one of my regulars." She reached out and began running her fingers through Kelsey's hair. "Wow, honey, you've got some problems here." She chuckled. "Trust me, it's gonna be worth it for you to wait. You really need help." She nodded toward her customer in the chair. "I'll probably be done with her in about an hour. You can wait—or if you want, you can come back around eleven."

"No, I can't wait, and I can't come back at eleven—I have to be at work at twelve," said Kelsey, increasingly annoyed. "That's why I made my appointment for ten o'clock."

"Suit yourself, sweetheart, but I could do wonders for you," Bebe called out as she turned and walked back to her station.

"Let's see what we have available next week and you can reschedule," said the receptionist, tapping his tablet.

"No, you don't understand. I'm not rescheduling," said Kelsey, incredulous. "You know, you have this beautiful place—I was really excited about coming here. But I can't believe the way you're treating a new customer. I'm not coming back—ever." She turned around and walked out.

As aggravated as she was, while pulling out of the parking lot Kelsey realized she now had time for a workout—and after that experience, she knew it would be a good one. She was glad she kept her gym bag in the trunk of her car. She could feel herself calming down and felt even better when she realized that even though she didn't have a new haircut, she did have a *not* Ideal Service story she could use to finish her homework assignment.

Kelsey was excited. She had a lot of points to discuss with Steven in their first Monday morning one-on-one chat before the regular team meeting. She knew he would be able to see what an important factor service was in the big picture of Ferguson's vs. ShopSmart, and she was eager to get the ball rolling and get Steven on board.

But the meeting room was empty when Kelsey arrived. After a few minutes, her teammate Rob walked in, followed soon by her other coworkers. At exactly eight-thirty, Steven hurried in and walked toward the front of the room, carrying a folder. When he looked up and saw Kelsey, he put his hands up in surrender, shook his head, and mouthed the words *I'm sorry*.

During the meeting, Kelsey could see that Steven was tense. He talked about the numbers being flat this week compared to last year, and he seemed to have more desperation in his voice when he mentioned ShopSmart.

After Steven had dismissed everyone, he walked up to Kelsey and said, "I'm sorry. I had a managers' meeting this morning, and I completely forgot that we were going to start getting together before the team meeting. I still want to hear about what you're learning and how you think it could help us—it's more important now than ever. I promise I'll meet you next week at 8:20—I'll put it on my calendar so that I don't forget." Steven looked at his watch. "I've got to go now, or I'll be late for another meeting. See you soon," he said as he hurried out of the room.

Kelsey was disappointed, but at least Steven still wanted to hear her ideas. He was obviously stressed, though—maybe it was about something he had learned in the managers' meeting. She wondered if her job was at risk.

Later that afternoon, Alex was taking Grandma Kate through her exercises at the clinic. At one point, he looked at Kelsey and said, "I hope you don't mind my asking, but is everything okay?"

Kelsey's eyes had been half focused on a chart on the wall as she thought about work. She was startled when Alex's question abruptly pulled her back into the present. "What? No! I mean yes!" She smiled and shook her head. "Sorry—I guess I was far away."

"Kelsey's been working too hard," said Grandma Kate. "She's learning about customer service in college and has figured out that the store where she works is terrible at it!"

"Grandma!" said Kelsey, with a laugh at her grandmother's brutal honesty.

"Actually, that's interesting," said Alex with a smile. "We talk about customer service a lot here at the clinic. Iris is pretty obsessed with it—and I mean that in a good way. I've learned a lot about service from her since I've been here. Good service is a lot simpler than people think."

"I know!" Kelsey exclaimed. "I can't believe how many businesses don't get that."

"It's just a matter of caring for and knowing your customers, clients, patients—whoever you're serving," said Alex. "It's about considering their needs and wanting to make them happy."

"I know!" repeated Kelsey. It was great to hear someone else say the same things she'd been thinking and hearing
about for weeks. Alex seemed to have as much enthusiasm for
the subject as she did.

"You should mention your situation to Iris next time
you're here. As a matter of fact," Alex turned to Grandma
Kate, "Iris will be working with you this Wednesday, Mrs.
Wilson, because I have another appointment."

"Thanks, Alex, I will talk to Iris," said Kelsey. "It would be
great to pick the brain of a business owner like her—especially
since you all obviously believe service is important. She must
be an amazing boss."

"She is," said Alex. "She'll be able to help you."

6

Culture of Service

"**I know you've** all been dying to know what the C in ICARE stands for, haven't you?" Professor Hartley asked as he looked around the class with a big grin on his face. He tapped his laptop and the screen read:

> I – **Ideal Service**
> C – **Culture of Service**
> A –
> R –
> E –

"The culture of any organization typically begins with a shared vision and shared values—and the organization's leaders need to make sure everyone knows what they are."

Kelsey noticed a man sitting in the front row, intently focused on what Professor Hartley was saying. She hadn't seen him in class before. Who was he?

"A true Culture of Service should include what we call a *service vision*, since every organization serves customers, whether the company is for-profit, nonprofit, or even in the public sector." The professor tapped the laptop once more to reveal a new slide that read:

> **Culture of Service:**
> Fostering an environment that
> focuses on serving the customer.

"The clearer an organization's service vision and values are, the easier it will be to create a strong service culture—because everyone in the organization will be focused on what's important and will know what behaviors are expected of them. It's also helpful for each person to have a clear vision of the kind of service they personally would like to deliver to their customer. As a service provider, what you *believe* about service will determine the kind of service you actually deliver." The professor paused.

"To explain further what I mean about Culture of Service, we have a special guest speaker today." Professor Hartley gestured toward the man sitting in the front row.

"Here to share a Legendary Service success story with you is a former colleague of mine and a good friend, Dan Murray.

Dan is the vice president of operations for ShopSmart and has been with the company for 12 years."

Surprised at the mention of ShopSmart, Kelsey instantly felt defensive.

The professor continued. "ShopSmart is going to open a new store in our area very soon, and Dan will be responsible for making sure everyone there is ready to provide Legendary Service beginning on day one. The people at ShopSmart have created an unbeatable service culture nationwide. They practice what I've been preaching to you about what great organizations do to stay competitive. Please join me in welcoming Dan Murray." The students applauded politely as Dan stood up to speak.

"Thanks for inviting me, Professor Hartley." Dan began to walk slowly back and forth in front of the room as he spoke.

"To piggyback on what Professor Hartley was saying, an organization's culture is made up of many things—people, history, vision, values, reputation, significant events, and even annual celebrations," Dan began. "Some of these things are deliberately cultivated, and others arise naturally. But a Culture of Service can exist only by *intention*—by creating a focus on the customer and holding everyone in the organization accountable for carrying out the service vision.

"Sometimes part of a company's culture can contribute positively to a service vision, such as managers having an open-door policy for their peers and direct reports. But other times, an aspect of the culture—even something like company history—actually can get in the way of delivering great service. This is especially true if senior leaders have a mentality of 'we've always done it that way; we don't need to change.'"

Kelsey's initial defensiveness had turned to attentiveness. As she listened to Dan's message, she quickly realized that the service culture at ShopSmart must be nothing like the service culture—or the *lack* of it—at Ferguson's.

Dan spoke to the class for a half hour, explaining how ShopSmart had created its service culture and how it had managed to sustain that culture over time.

"Let me summarize some key ideas for you to think about as you go back to your own organizations," Dan said as he finished his presentation. "To have a true Culture of Service, you need to have the following in place: senior management buy-in and support; all employees trained in Legendary Service— what it is, what it looks and feels like, and how to provide it; and a sustainability plan that includes follow-up activities, goals focused on service, and methods to measure progress."

After Dan sat down, Professor Hartley thanked him and gave the students their assignment for the week. "I want you to look for two different organizations that demonstrate they have a Culture of Service and write a piece about them for our next class. Think about your own workplace—do you know your company's vision or values? Does your organization have a service vision? If you don't know, ask your supervisor. It's fine for one of your examples to be your own company, if it fits the description."

I wish I could use Ferguson's as one of my examples, but that's not going to happen, thought Kelsey.

She stayed in her seat for a moment as the class stood up to leave. She was so impressed with what Dan had shared, she found herself wishing she could work at ShopSmart instead of Ferguson's. She approached him as the class filed out of the room.

"Hi, Mr. Murray. I really enjoyed your presentation. My name's Kelsey Young," she said as she shook his hand.

"Hi, Kelsey. Please call me Dan."

"I work for Ferguson's, one of your competitors, and it makes me sad to admit we don't have anything close to the kind of culture you have at ShopSmart."

"Oh, yes, I know a lot about Ferguson's," said Dan. He immediately switched gears to talk about ShopSmart again. "I'm proud of our culture—it helps our customers feel valued so that they know how much we appreciate them. Without our external customers, we wouldn't be in business. But we also know we're only as good as each of our internal customers— our associates—so we try to acknowledge their efforts as much as we can."

"I wish we had that same environment," lamented Kelsey.

"Have you talked to your manager about making improvements in your store? Sometimes you have to take baby steps and work up to the bigger ones."

"Actually, I've talked to my department manager, Steven Walker. He seems interested in my ideas, but he's as frustrated as I am. I don't get the feeling the senior managers really care. They seem a lot more concerned about numbers than about keeping customers happy—internal *or* external."

"Don't give up too soon, Kelsey. If you want to stay with Ferguson's, keep working toward making changes you believe are for the good of the company, the customers, and the employees. You never know how much influence you might have."

"I'll keep trying. It was really nice meeting you, Mr. Murray—I mean, Dan. Thank you again." Kelsey shook his hand again and smiled.

She walked to the parking lot with a renewed commitment to help Steven improve their department. *If only the senior managers would buy into the concept of a service culture,* she thought. But she'd never seen any evidence that they cared about vision, values, or a Culture of Service. All they seemed to be focused on were sales, profits, and the bottom line. The worst thing was that they didn't appear to understand the connection between the two.

The next day at Ferguson's, Kelsey looked around in the break room and the meeting room and saw nothing posted about vision or values. As it happened, Steven was on the floor helping out, since they were still busy with Back to School shoppers. When there was a lull in the action that afternoon, Kelsey brought up the subject with him.

"We do have a company vision, but I don't remember it exactly," said Steven. "It's something like 'Be the Leader in Providing Quality Merchandise at Affordable Prices.'"

Kelsey quickly told Steven what she'd learned in class about organizations that create a service vision to help build a Culture of Service and encourage that mindset in every employee.

"That does make a lot of sense," said Steven. "If we had a memorable service vision posted in our break room and we talked about it in our weekly department meetings, people could have it in mind while they were helping customers."

They talked for a few more minutes until Kelsey had to turn away to greet some customers who had walked into the department. As she turned, Steven said, "Why don't you take a shot at putting together a service vision that I could share at my next managers' meeting?"

Great, she thought as she walked toward the customers. *Why did I open my big mouth? What do I know about creating a service vision?*

▲ ★ ★ ☆ ★ ★ ▲

That afternoon at the clinic, before she escorted Grandma Kate to the therapy room, Iris turned to Kelsey and said, "Kelsey, could you come back with us? I want to show you how you can work with your grandmother between our sessions to help strengthen her wrist."

As they were walking through the door to the back hallway, Kelsey happened to look up. She couldn't believe she'd missed seeing the sign above the door when she'd been in the office before. It read:

> ## Our Service Vision
> To treat our patients as family
> and nurture them back to health.

"I just noticed the sign about your service vision," said Kelsey as the three women sat down in the treatment room. "Your vision really describes the business you're in. My professor was just talking about this in my customer service class yesterday."

"And you're at State. Don't tell me you have Professor Hartley?" Iris asked, surprised.

"Yes—how did you know?"

"Because I took his Legendary Service course when I was there! It was one of my required business courses. It's a small world—or maybe it's just a small town," Iris said, smiling.

"That's amazing!" exclaimed Kelsey. "Alex told us he's learned a lot about service from you. It's great to know that you learned from the same person who's teaching me."

"That course was where I learned the importance of creating a Culture of Service," Iris continued. "When I started this business, I shared the concept of a service vision with my new team, and we worked together to create one for the clinic. Now everyone who works here is clear about the business we're in and how they're all expected to serve our customers. We strive to be consistent in our service and always keep the patient top of mind."

"Well, from what I've seen, you're all living your service vision. It's great to see it in action. I only wish I knew how to do the same thing where I work," said Kelsey.

"I'd be happy to talk with you about it, if you'd like," said Iris. "Service is one of my true passions. I believe great service, or the lack of it, can make or break a business. I'm no expert on the topic—but what I learned in my business courses, I've implemented in my organization, and it's worked for me."

"It's so nice of you to offer   I really appreciate any help you can give me," said Kelsey gratefully. "My boss just gave me the task of coming up with a service vision for our store, and I have no idea where to start."

"It's a good sign if you're getting some management buy-in—that's absolutely necessary in a larger organization."

Kelsey was delighted at the idea of having a mentor like Iris, who had applied all the components of Legendary Service to her own thriving business. She couldn't think of a better way to reinforce everything she was learning in her course and at the same time get some real-world tips she could use at Ferguson's. What a lucky break!

At the end of Grandma Kate's session, Kelsey and Iris agreed to meet the following Saturday morning at a nearby café.

On the way home from the clinic, Kelsey made a quick stop to pick up a pizza she'd ordered, while Grandma Kate waited in the car. As the cashier was preparing to run Kelsey's card through the machine, his manager walked up and said, "Ryan, are you the one who sliced the pepperoni this morning?"

The cashier froze in place, looked at the manager, and said, "Yes—why?"

"Because the meat slicer wasn't cleaned properly." The manager raised her voice as she continued. "*You have to clean the meat slicer after you slice the meat!*"

The cashier and the manager turned their backs on Kelsey and began to speak in low tones. It was clear that the cashier was being reprimanded. Kelsey had the pizza box in her hands, but the cashier was still holding her credit card.

After a few minutes of feeling completely invisible, Kelsey started to speak: "Excuse me—" At that moment, the manager stopped talking to the cashier and walked briskly back into the kitchen area. The cashier turned to face Kelsey and finished the transaction silently. His face was red. Kelsey couldn't tell whether it was from anger, embarrassment, or both.

She couldn't believe that neither of the two—especially the manager—had bothered to acknowledge her or to apologize for making her stand and wait through their dramatic scene while she held her cooling pizza. She decided not to say anything to the cashier. He'd been lectured enough for one day.

Kelsey made sure she got to the café early on Saturday morning and had her questions ready for Iris, who pulled into the parking lot right behind her. As they sat and talked, Kelsey heard Iris say virtually the same things Professor Hartley had said in class about creating a service culture—including establishing clear values.

"At the clinic, the team and I worked together to decide what our values would be. The first is *Integrity in All Things*, then comes *Quality Care*, after that is *Relationships*, and the final one is *Learning*," said Iris.

"Why only four values?" asked Kelsey. "I would think you'd want to have at least eight or ten."

"Organizations that have too many values often find that people can only focus on a few. The values they focus on need to be the ones that really impact behavior. Actually, we started with twelve, but we knew we would be cutting them down to only three or four. It was a bit difficult for us as a team to decide among some of them. I actually had to arm-wrestle Barbara to get my favorite one, Learning, in there—and I won!" Iris said with an impish smile.

Kelsey sighed. "My company has so much work to do in this whole process. I know if the senior managers at Ferguson's realized how little it might take to get the employees on board with creating a service culture at the store, they would want to do it. Professor Hartley said you need to start with your employees, because they are your *internal* customers. But I'm sure our managers have never thought of the employees that way."

She told Iris about Dan Murray from ShopSmart talking to her class.

"ShopSmart knows how to treat its people as customers. It's the kind of leadership I wish our store had," said Kelsey. "Mr. Murray made service sound simple and fun—and obviously having a Culture of Service is one of the things that makes ShopSmart so successful. I feel as if my boss, Steven, and I are the only ones at Ferguson's who actually care about our customers."

"Professor Hartley and Mr. Murray are right," said Iris. "Establishing a Culture of Service has to begin internally. Maybe Steven could start each staff meeting with praise for a teammate he caught giving good service to a customer or helping a coworker. If he wants the focus to be on serving customers, he needs to praise his people—his internal customers—for that behavior. Keep working with him and encouraging him, Kelsey. You really can make a difference."

Kelsey nodded thoughtfully, then checked her watch and realized she had to leave for work in a few minutes. She stood up and held out her hand to Iris.

"Thank you so much, Iris, for your time and ideas. I really appreciate your willingness to mentor me," said Kelsey as Iris shook her hand.

"Kelsey, I just had a thought. Are you a baseball fan?"

"I am—and my grandma is a huge fan, too," said Kelsey.

"That's great to hear, because tomorrow is Move Right Clinic's 'team day' at the park. We do it every year as one of our team-building field trips, and we actually have a couple of tickets that were going to go unused. If you want to see a place that has an incredible service culture, and if you and your grandma are free tomorrow, I want you to come to the baseball park as our guests. They're even going to flash our clinic's name on the giant screen!"

"Thank you—that sounds like a lot of fun! And I have the day off tomorrow," said Kelsey. "My grandma is going to be thrilled. We haven't been able to get to a game yet this season."

"When they built the new park a few years ago, they implemented a huge guest services program that included a vision and values for the team, the park, and all of its employees," said Iris. "The service culture is obvious there—you can see it in every park employee you meet."

They arranged the time and place where they would meet up the next day and said their goodbyes. Kelsey was excited to tell Grandma Kate they would be going to the ball game tomorrow. She drove to work with fresh motivation to put more new ideas into practice.

Steven called Kelsey and two of her coworkers together just before the store opened. "Unfortunately, our store had seven people quit this week, and two of them were from our department—Patrick and Amy. Management has a freeze on filling those positions right now, so it will just be the three of you in the department today. I'll be here on the floor helping as much as I can. It's going to be a busy day, so we all need to pull together and work as a team." Steven was putting on a brave face, but he was clearly feeling the stress of the situation.

"Are they going to fill those positions soon? How long is the freeze supposed to last?" asked Kelsey.

"That's all the information I was given," said Steven, shaking his head. "I'm really sorry, but let's try to make the best of it for now."

The rest of the day was very busy, just as Steven had predicted, and the customers were irritated with the long lines. A Saturday during Back to School season was not a good time to be short-staffed. Steven, Kelsey, and the rest of the team buckled down and did the best they could, but the atmosphere in the store was sour.

"I can't believe they don't have more people working on a Saturday afternoon," a man said as he walked past Kelsey.

"ShopSmart can't open soon enough," said the woman walking next to him.

After Saturday's difficult day at work, Kelsey was glad to have something fun to do on Sunday. She and Grandma Kate met Iris, Alex, and the rest of the clinic staff at the entrance to the baseball park.

As they passed through the security checkpoint, one of the guards saw Grandma Kate's big handbag and, smiling, said to her coworker, "That looks like the kind of bag Mary Poppins had. We'd better check it closely—she might have a lamp in there!"

"I have to bring my big bag—it's the only one my mitt will fit in," said Grandma Kate, pulling the mitt out of her bag as one of the guards looked inside.

The other guard pointed to the mitt and said, "How many foul balls have you caught with that mitt?"

"None yet, but I'm going to go down trying!" Grandma Kate joked.

Kelsey couldn't help but notice the security guards' fun and warm interaction with Grandma Kate, despite the fact that they were doing a very serious job—protecting the safety of the fans.

When they got to their seats, Grandma Kate said to the stadium usher, "I'm so glad we got here early. I hate missing the first pitch."

"Yes, ma'am, I'm glad you're here early, too," said the usher with a smile. "I see you brought your mitt. These seats are in a great place to catch foul balls—good luck!"

"I love baseball," said Iris to Kelsey as they all settled into their seats. "I try to come to as many of the Sunday games as I can. The staff here really knows how to make the fans feel welcome and important."

As Kelsey looked out on the field, she noticed a large sign attached to the scoreboard. The park's logo was at the top, and below it were the words *We're in the Business of Creating Major League Memories.*

Iris noticed Kelsey looking at the sign. "Every person who works here makes it their mission to create memorable experiences for the fans," she said.

"Well, so far it's working for me," said Kelsey, impressed by what she'd already experienced.

As Iris was talking with Kelsey, a well-dressed man approached and stopped at the row where they were sitting. Iris noticed him, smiled, and said, "Kelsey and Kate, I want you to meet Reggie Aldersen. He's the head of operations here at the stadium and a good friend of mine. Kelsey, I told Reggie you were studying customer service and might want to hear how the park originally established its service culture."

Kelsey shook Reggie's hand. "I noticed your vision statement on the scoreboard," she said.

Reggie smiled and said, "When the park opened five years ago, we wanted to make sure everyone in the stadium—employees and visitors—understood our service vision and values. We put all our people through customer service training, invited their best thoughts, and even launched an internal website where we could continue to capture their feedback and celebrate their successes.

"You can see that our service vision is to create major league memories. If we do a good job making memories for the fans, we hope, when they're leaving the park, they'll talk about who they're going to bring to the game next time. In other words, they'll have had such a great time here, they'll want to share it with others."

"I remember the first time I came here," said Alex. "I was with my brother and his boys, who are eight and ten. When we were leaving the park, one of my nephews said, 'Dad, next time we come, can I bring my friend Matthew? He'd really like it.'"

"Your staff seems to understand how to help people relax and enjoy themselves," said Grandma Kate. "Even your security guards know how to create positive memories."

"I'm glad you noticed," said Reggie. "To be sure our vision and values really sank in with our people, at the end of our very first game, after the fans had left, we took everyone—both frontline and behind-the-scenes staff—down on the playing field and had them walk the bases."

"That must have blown their minds," said Grandma Kate.

"They loved it," said Reggie, smiling. "At each base was a sign with one of our four rank-ordered values. At first base, the sign read: *Safety—Our Number One Value*. We know if one of our fans gets carried out of the park on a stretcher, it won't be a great major league memory."

"That's for sure!" exclaimed Grandma Kate.

"At second base was a sign that read: *Service—Our Number Two Value*."

"What was at third base?" asked Kelsey, who was getting into the conversation.

"*Fun—Our Number Three Value*," said Reggie. "That was suggested by one of our frontline folks. She said, 'Remember when you were young and went on a date? If you didn't have any fun, what were the chances that your date had fun and would want to go out with you again?'"

"Zip," said Grandma Kate, laughing. "But if you had fun, your date probably had fun, too."

"That's right," said Reggie. "So if we as customer service providers—even the security guards—are having fun, it increases the odds that our fans will also have fun and that they'll want to come back."

"What's your fourth value?" Kelsey asked.

"At home plate, the sign read: *Success—Our Number Four Value.* That's all about operating a profitable, well-run organization. After all, this isn't only about having fun. But since Success is our fourth-ranked value, we won't do anything to save money that might put people in danger. And we won't downsize our staff in the park, because it would be hard for people to have a memorable time if they couldn't find anyone to serve them."

"That's interesting—having your values rank ordered," observed Kelsey.

"We think it's important because sometimes value conflicts occur. For example, suppose one of our ushers was helping you with something and heard a scream that wasn't coming from the field. That usher would probably turn and run toward the scream—because our number one value, Safety, was calling."

"I get it," said Kelsey. "That makes a lot of sense."

"This is why I wanted you to come to a game, Kelsey," said Iris. "They really do it right here. In fact, Reggie told me that the first summer the park was in business, they got 7,500 e-mails and letters from fans with stories of how impressed they were by the great customer service."

"Wow! I can see why," said Kelsey.

With that, Reggie said his goodbyes and headed off.

Kelsey and Grandma Kate decided to get some food before the game began. Alex had a list in his hand and offered to walk with Kelsey to the food court. "I get to be everyone's personal hot dog vendor today," he said with a laugh as they walked up the steps.

Kelsey ordered two chicken taco salads with sodas as Alex went to the next window for hot dogs and drinks for the clinic team. After they got back to their seats, Kelsey opened the bag containing the salads and removed the lid from one of the bowls.

"Darn it," she muttered to Grandma Kate. "They got my order wrong. This salad has beef, not chicken, on it." She checked, and Grandma Kate's salad was the same. "Oh, well. . . ."

Alex looked over and said, "Kelsey, take it back and tell them your order is wrong. I'm sure they'll make it right."

"That's okay," Kelsey said, thinking of the scene between the pizza cashier and his manager. She didn't want anyone to get in trouble.

Alex stood up. "Come on—I'll go with you. Let's see if they really care about their customers here, like they say they do."

Kelsey reluctantly agreed and walked with Alex back to the food court. She approached the same worker who had helped her earlier.

"I'm sorry, but I ordered chicken taco salads, and these are beef," Kelsey said quietly as she put the food on the counter in front of him.

"I'm the one who's sorry," said the young man, swiftly removing the salads from sight. "I'll get you two chicken taco salads right away."

In less than a minute, he was back with two fresh salads and two other packages, all of which he slipped into a large bag.

"I'm including an order of chips and guacamole on the house," he said.

"Oh, thanks—but you don't have to do that," said Kelsey.

"It's the least we can do when you had to make an extra trip."

"See? I knew they'd make it right," said Alex as they turned to walk back.

Just before rounding the corner to go down the stairs to their seats, Kelsey stopped as she noticed a sign on the wall that had a picture of a baseball diamond. The logo of the park was in the center of the diamond, and below it were the words *Hitting a Guest Services Home Run!* Each of the bases had a word printed on it. The word on first base was *Safety*; on second base, *Service*; on third base, *Fun*; and on home plate, *Success*.

"This is cool," said Kelsey. "Their rank-ordered values are right here on the sign for everyone to see."

"They're serious about service here," said Alex.

"Iris," Kelsey said as they reached their seats, "you were right—this place is really special."

Toward the end of the game, Iris said, "Kelsey, get your grandma's mitt ready and watch this!" Grandma Kate quickly handed Kelsey her baseball mitt.

Iris waved at the peanut vendor coming up the aisle, catching his eye. Even though he was six or eight rows away, he flipped a bag of peanuts up behind his back and lobbed it over people's heads directly at the mitt Kelsey was holding high. The bag landed on target with a comfortable *thump*. Everyone around them cheered.

"Hey, no foul balls today, Kelsey, but you did a great job catching those peanuts," said Grandma Kate with a laugh.

That night, Kelsey was so inspired by what she'd learned and observed at the baseball park she did an online search for *service vision statements*. Finding several examples, she started jotting down ideas for Ferguson's service vision. She also made a few notes of things she wanted to share with Steven and sent him a quick e-mail to remind him they'd agreed to get together the next morning before the department meeting. She hoped he could make time to see her this week.

Kelsey arrived a half hour before the department meeting on Monday and was glad to see Steven walk into the meeting room moments later.

"Okay, Kelsey, I need some good news," Steven said as they sat down at the table. "Give me the highlights about what you've been learning and maybe we can get some positive momentum going around here."

"I'm getting some good ideas for Ferguson's service vision," Kelsey said. "I think we need to picture our people interacting with our customers and think about what we offer customers that causes them to come back. Here's what I came up with: *To Provide Genuine Value and Caring Service to Every Customer, Every Day.* What do you think?"

"Hmmm . . . " said Steven as he wrote down the phrase and paused to read it again. "'To Provide Genuine Value and Caring Service to Every Customer, Every Day.'" He looked up at Kelsey and smiled. "I like it! I'll take this to the next managers' meeting and present it as our store's potential new service vision. Once I get it approved by management, we'll put up a couple of signs stating the vision so that employees can read them when they come to work and when they go on their breaks."

Kelsey was encouraged that Steven liked what she had written. "You could also put a sign in the front of the store where customers can see it," she suggested. She told Steven about the vision and values statements posted at the baseball park.

Steven was getting animated. "That's another good idea. What if we also put a few morale-building plaques around the break room with messages like *Our People Make the Difference* or *You Are Our Number One Priority*? Do you think that would make employees feel more valued?"

Kelsey flinched. "The only problem with messages like those is that senior management would need to back them up with action," she said. "Feel-good plaques don't mean anything to employees unless they know their leaders stand behind what the sign is saying."

"Ouch," said Steven. "I hate to admit it, but you're right. Behavior should always precede plaques!"

"That goes for the service vision signs, too. You'll probably need to get people talking about the meaning of our service vision at our weekly meetings so that everyone gets it into their heads," said Kelsey. "And that's just part of creating a service culture. It's about continuously focusing on the customer and holding everyone in the company responsible for applying the vision and values. Speaking of values—could you ask at the next managers' meeting if Ferguson's has a posted list of values?"

"It would be crazy if we didn't," said Steven, "but I've never heard anyone talk about that."

Then, although she wasn't sure she should, Kelsey told Steven about Dan Murray from ShopSmart coming to talk to her class and the impression he had made on her.

Steven looked serious. "I've heard about Dan Murray—he's one of the main reasons ShopSmart is so successful. No wonder our store management is nervous about ShopSmart opening down the street. Those people walk their talk."

"He obviously knows what he's talking about," said Kelsey, "and he made it sound so simple. He also was really helpful and open with his advice when I talked to him about Ferguson's."

Steven looked a little uncomfortable. "I hope you didn't give away any of our trade secrets!" he said with a nervous laugh.

"I just don't understand how our senior managers can't see the value of focusing more on service and less on cutting costs," Kelsey replied. "And now there's a *hiring freeze*? I know I'm not a manager, Steven, but with ShopSmart opening, it seems to me that right now is absolutely the *worst* time for us to put a freeze on new hires."

"Kelsey, I'm getting an idea of my own. I want you to write up everything you're learning. Let's work together on a presentation for senior management, but not just a service vision—a complete customer service initiative. I think the time is right for Ferguson's to step up as a real competitor for ShopSmart. And one of the first things we need to do is to start emulating their service culture."

"That's a great idea! I'll help you in any way I can," Kelsey agreed enthusiastically.

"You know," said Steven as he rose from his chair, "I've been in management here for five years, and I've never heard anyone talk about customer service the way you do, Kelsey. I'm really impressed with your passion for this. With this kind of attitude and determination, I think you're going to go a long way in the company."

I'll believe that when I see it, thought Kelsey. But she just smiled and said, "Thanks."

Attentiveness

O n Tuesday morning, Kelsey watched with interest as Professor Hartley called the students' attention to the words on the projection screen:

> I – Ideal Service
> C – Culture of Service
> A – Attentiveness
> R –
> E –

"Once an organization has clearly identified its service vision," the professor began, "the next step is to get clear on who its customers are and what they want. This is called being *attentive* to customers." He tapped on his laptop and revealed the next slide.

> **Attentiveness:**
> Knowing your customers
> and their preferences.

"I'd like each of you to make a list, right now, of all the different types of customers your company, or a company you might like to work for, serves. I'll give you six minutes."

Kelsey quickly jotted down every kind of Ferguson's customer she could think of. Her list read:

- Parents shopping for kids' school supplies and clothes

- Teens needing high school or college supplies, clothes, electronics, or sporting goods

- Adults looking for clothes, electronics, office supplies, or sporting goods

- Customers with different income levels

The professor started walking around the room. "As you look at your list, think about this: Do all of these customers have the same preferences and needs? Or, to put it another way, would you treat all of these customers the same way?"

He glanced at Kelsey's list. "Kelsey, you wrote *teens* and also *parents shopping for their kids* as two different types of customers you deal with. Do you treat those types of customers the same way?"

"No, not at all," replied Kelsey. "I mean, I'm polite and respectful to them both, but I talk differently to parents than I do to teenagers."

"And why is that? Why do you talk differently to them?"

"I guess with teenagers, I try to relate to what I was interested in at that age so that I can connect with them. With the parents, I try to draw out of them what they think their kids need for going back to school and make suggestions. If the parents already know what they need, I like to help them find it fast, since they tend to be on a tighter time schedule than teenagers."

"That's a great example. Thanks," said Professor Hartley. "What Kelsey just explained, whether she realizes this or not, is something that many successful companies do to get to know their customers better. It's called *customer profiling*. Customer profiling is a great way for people in an organization to get to know the different types of customers they serve and those customers' specific preferences. That way, they can make sure they are not only meeting each customer's individual needs but also looking for ways to continuously improve the service they are providing."

The professor asked the class to turn to a page in their textbook titled *Customer Profile Questions*.

"Let's do some real work in class with this activity. I'd like you to take some time to answer a few questions about both your internal and external customers. Keep in mind, *internal customers* refers to other people or departments within your own organization that you and your department might serve. For instance, do you need to fill out paperwork on your inventory for another department, or to get reimbursed for something? Pick either a department or a person and answer the questions as they relate to that department or person.

"When you're finished with that page, answer the same questions about an external customer. As you can see, you need to think about what this customer requires from you, what your typical responses are, and ways in which you can exceed their expectations. What could you teach them that would inspire their loyalty? How will you measure your success? Go back to the list you wrote down a few minutes ago and pick one of those types of customers to write about."

As Kelsey was working on the assignment, she found it interesting to think about colleagues who worked in other departments within her store—like her friend Rachel in the jewelry department—and recognize that they were her customers, too. She'd never stopped to think about that before. When she got to the external customer section, she noticed that the answers she came up with while thinking of one type of customer were completely different from those she wrote when she thought of a different type of customer.

"Now that you've had some time to jot down your thoughts, choose a partner and share your answers. This will take a few minutes, but you'll find it interesting to hear how diverse other people's customers can be."

The students began to move around and compare notes. Kelsey turned to the person next to her, a middle-aged man named Hank who had retired from the military a few years ago and opened a small neighborhood bar.

"Why don't you go ahead, since I already gave my example," suggested Kelsey.

"Okay," said Hank. "So, in my bar, I've got this customer named Mark who comes in two or three times a week after he gets off work. He always sits at the bar. Mark's requirement of me? Usually a beer. Ha!" Hank laughed and looked at the book for the next question. Kelsey smiled—Hank obviously enjoyed his job.

"Okay, so my typical response is to give Mark a beer and listen while he complains about his job. The way I try to exceed his expectations is to be sure I remember to call him by name—Mark—and give him a cold glass and a coaster for his beer. One time he asked for some popcorn, so now I put a bowl of popcorn on the bar when I see him walk in. What can I teach him? I guess I could teach him about the different draft beers we carry, because he always orders the same kind. Maybe I could start giving him a sample of a different kind of beer every time he comes in. He might like that." Hank looked down at the book again. "And the way I measure my success with Mark is that he keeps coming back two or three times a week, sometimes with a buddy. Yesterday he even talked about bringing in his bowling team after their next league match."

"So are all of your customers pretty similar to Mark?" Kelsey asked.

"Oh, no," said Hank. "For instance, there's a nice young couple I've seen in the bar a few times on Saturday afternoons. They sit back in the corner at a table with their computers. I think they might be writers. They like it that we've got free Wi-Fi. They usually order wine and stay a couple of hours. They like those little bar pretzels better than popcorn, so I give them a bowl of those."

After most of the students had finished sharing with their partners, the professor ended the class with a very interesting thought that stayed with Kelsey.

"Remember—Attentiveness to customers is not only knowing each of them and their personal preferences, but also paying attention to the impression *you* are making on *them*. You probably have heard about the importance of first impressions."

At that moment, Kelsey could hear her mother saying, "You never get a second chance to make a first impression."

"The interesting thing is this—research shows it's the *last* impression you make that can actually shape and define someone's entire experience. Everything can go great throughout a business transaction, but if the last interaction a customer has with you is bad, it can cancel out their entire positive experience up to that point."

Kelsey immediately remembered the hair salon—she had been so impressed at first, but just a few minutes later, she had walked out, never to return.

"For homework, I'd like you to go online and find two organizations that do customer profiling. Research how they use that information to their customers' advantage when serving them. Write up two pages and submit them to me before class. Also, just for fun, as you go through the week, pay attention to the *first* and also the *last* impression you have when you get service—and think about which impression really defines your experience."

Because Alex was running late for Grandma Kate's therapy appointment, Barbara offered Kelsey and Grandma Kate refreshments while they waited. "We have coffee, tea, soda, or water, if you're interested."

"I'd love a cup of tea if it's not too much trouble," Grandma Kate said.

"No trouble at all. Choose one you'd like." Barbara opened a beautiful box displaying 10 different varieties of tea bags.

"Mmmmm—I'd like the chai, please," said Grandma Kate after studying her choices.

"My pleasure. It will be just a few minutes. And for you, Kelsey? I know you usually have a water bottle with you. Would you like one?"

"I'd love one—thank you. I was in such a rush today, I forgot to grab mine."

Barbara came back moments later, carrying hot tea in a pretty china cup and a cold bottle of water.

"Alex should be here in about five minutes. The road construction slowed everyone down today. I'm sorry you have to wait."

Grandma Kate turned to Kelsey and said, "I don't mind waiting at all when I have a good cup of tea. And look—they serve it in a china teacup!"

The receptionist and Kelsey smiled at each other. Kelsey was amazed at how the clinic seemed to know the little things that would make an 80-year-old woman happy.

"I'm so sorry to keep you waiting, ladies," Alex said as he burst through the door a few minutes later. He approached Grandma Kate with outstretched hands. "Let me carry your tea for you as we go to the back." He turned to Kelsey and said with a grin, "How are you doing, Kelsey? Still reliving that great peanut catch?"

"Very funny," Kelsey said, and smiled.

The atmosphere at Kelsey's store had been tense for several days. Senior managers had been either on the sales floor barking orders at the employees or in meetings. Kelsey wondered if they were getting more nervous because ShopSmart's opening was now imminent. She tried to talk to Steven a few times when things were slow in her department, but he was preoccupied and didn't seem to have time for her—and he'd canceled their pre-meeting huddle for Monday.

In the department meeting Monday morning, Kelsey found out why Steven had been on edge.

"We're going to have a visitor in our store today," said Steven. "Eric Glatch, our vice president of operations, is going to be making the rounds through every department and then meeting with the store management team. As you know, sales have been pretty flat for a while and customer complaints have been increasing, so they're sending in the big dogs to see what's going on. With ShopSmart opening soon, the corporate office is concerned about our store's numbers. Here's the good news—Home and Office is the only department that has increased sales and hasn't had any customer complaints!"

At this, Steven began to clap his hands, and soon everyone was applauding and smiling.

"You deserve the applause—you're all doing a great job. I know you've been working harder, and I can see you coming together better as a team. I really appreciate that, especially since we've been so shorthanded. I've noticed better attitudes these last few weeks, too—and I know you're all going to put your best foot forward today when Mr. Glatch is here. I'll be on the floor with you most of the day. Let's make sure every shelf is stocked and you're all wearing your name badges."

As everyone was leaving the meeting, Kelsey overheard Rob and Darla talking.

"It's cool that Steven recognizes how hard we've been working. It feels good to know he's paying attention," said Rob.

"Yeah, Steven's great, but one of the assistant store managers came up to me last week and bit my head off about a messy display," said Darla.

"Hey, guys," Kelsey joined in. "Let's do whatever it takes to really impress our customers today. Maybe the senior management team and Mr. Glatch will notice."

Rob and Darla agreed. Last week, Kelsey had heard Steven praising Rob for working harder and being more pleasant with customers. Even if people on the Home and Office team weren't getting recognition from upper management, they were getting more respect from Steven—and their attitudes were improving as a result.

It was obvious who Mr. Glatch was when he finally showed up in Kelsey's department just before lunchtime, since all the senior managers were walking in a group behind him. Everyone looked very serious. One of the managers introduced him to Steven.

"Nice to see you again, Mr. Glatch," said Steven as he turned to approach his team. "Let me introduce you to a few of my team members. This is Darla, Rob, and Kelsey."

Each of them smiled and said "Hello" quietly when Steven said their name. Rob and Kelsey put out their hands to shake Mr. Glatch's hand.

"Hello," Mr. Glatch said coldly, with a broad wave of his arm.

"Our department's sales numbers are ahead of plan by 4 percent. I'm also proud to report that our team here in Home and Office has had zero customer complaints this quarter," said Steven. "As a matter of fact, we received a customer letter complimenting us on Kelsey's excellent service."

Kelsey smiled confidently. Mr. Glatch looked very stern as he raised his finger and pointed at Kelsey, Rob, and Darla, in turn.

"You all need to know that the office supply and home décor departments at ShopSmart are very popular," he said. "We can't afford to lose one customer to the competition—not *one* customer. Remember that." He turned abruptly and walked away, the managers clustered behind him.

"Now *that* was inspiring," Rob said sarcastically after Mr. Glatch was out of earshot.

"Sure makes *me* want to work harder," joked Darla.

Kelsey couldn't get over how different Mr. Glatch was from Dan Murray, the man from ShopSmart who had spoken to her class. They had the same title—vice president of operations—but they were worlds apart in their leadership styles. She was sure Mr. Murray would have found some way to compliment each team member. Mr. Glatch's behavior, on the other hand, was unfriendly—almost threatening. *How could that kind of leader inspire anyone?* she wondered.

★★★★★

8

Responsiveness

Kelsey walked into the classroom a few minutes early on Tuesday, hoping to catch her professor before the other students arrived. He was sitting at the desk, looking at his computer.

"Hi, Kelsey. You're here early," Professor Hartley said as he stood up.

"I'd hoped to talk with you for a few minutes before class started," Kelsey began. "I was just wondering how well you know Mr. Murray. I think you said you'd worked with him; is that right?"

"Yes, we worked together when we were in college, but we go back even further than that," said the professor. "We actually grew up together in the Midwest and have stayed good friends all these years. Why do you ask?"

"Yesterday at work, we had a visit from the vice president of operations for Ferguson's. He has the same title as Mr. Murray, but they're nothing alike. Mr. Glatch was so tough and uncaring. He didn't even acknowledge the things we'd been doing well. Mr. Murray seems so positive and down to earth. Is he that way around his employees?"

"Absolutely. Remember what I said to the class on the very first day of the semester?"

Kelsey thought for a moment. "You mean the part about relationships?"

"Exactly. It's how you treat people—in this case, internal customers—that makes them feel valued. You didn't feel that Mr. Glatch cared about you or your coworkers or that he appreciated your hard work. Dan understands the importance of making sure his people are recognized and praised for their efforts. If they know they're appreciated, they'll pass along those positive feelings to their customers."

Kelsey stood in silence.

"Kelsey, have you thought about working at ShopSmart? I think you'd fit in well with the culture there. I'd be happy to call Dan for you if you think it might help." The professor had read Kelsey's mind. She was surprised by his offer—but she wasn't ready to make that leap quite yet.

"Thanks, Dr. Hartley. That's really nice of you. I'll think about it."

Just then, a few other people walked into the room, laughing and talking.

"Sounds good, Kelsey. Just let me know."

Professor Hartley started off the class with a quick review of what they'd learned so far about Legendary Service, including the definitions of Ideal Service, Culture of Service, and Attentiveness—the first three segments of the ICARE model.

"Now I'm going to put you all on the spot," the professor said. "Who has a good service story that can illustrate any of the concepts we've learned so far?"

A woman in the back of the room raised her hand.

"Thank you, Connie. Please stand up and tell us your story."

Looking a bit uncomfortable, Connie stood up. "A couple of weeks ago I was picking up some takeout for dinner. As I was standing at the counter waiting for my order, I got a call on my cell phone. Even though I was talking quietly, I think it was obvious to the woman behind the counter that I wasn't happy with the person on the other end of the line. When I hung up, she looked at me and said, 'Tough day?' very sincerely. I said, 'Yes.' I paid, and she handed me my order—and then she looked me straight in the eye and said, 'I hope you have a fabulous weekend.' It was such a small thing, but I felt as if she truly cared about me and how I was feeling. I actually walked out of there feeling better because of her."

"Thanks, Connie," the professor said as he turned to the class. "When you are the service provider, a simple word or gesture on your part is sometimes all that's needed to show customers that you're in tune with them and you care about them as people, not just as customers. That kind of connection can instantly create customer loyalty.

"This is a great way to make the transition into the next segment in the ICARE model." He tapped his laptop, and the words on the screen read:

> I – **Ideal Service**
> C – **Culture of Service**
> A – **Attentiveness**
> R – **Responsiveness**
> E –

"Being responsive to your customers goes hand in hand with being attentive to their needs and preferences," said the professor as he tapped once more to show the next slide.

> **Responsiveness:**
> Demonstrating a genuine
> willingness to serve others
> as you fulfill their individual needs.

"I want you all to think of a time when you were the customer and you felt that a service provider was truly focused on you. Write down everything the person did that made you feel as if they wanted to help you and wanted to meet or exceed your expectations."

He gave the students a few minutes to write, then asked them to call out their answers.

"He listened to my concerns and needs."

"She took care of my problem right away."

"She made me feel cared about—like she was on my side."

"Those are all great examples," said the professor. "Being a good listener, dealing with difficult situations, and caring for your customers are all parts of Responsiveness.

"Now think about someone you know who is a good listener. What is it about them that makes you put them in this category?"

Kelsey immediately thought of her grandma. When she was younger, she would stay with her grandma for a month every summer. Her grandma knew how to ask questions about school or friends that would get Kelsey talking. She would sometimes respond with comments such as, "That sounds like fun," to let Kelsey know she was listening. Those conversations had always made Kelsey feel special. She smiled as she realized that her grandma was still doing the same thing these days—asking about her work, school, and friends, and always being there to listen. She still seemed to be truly interested in everything that was going on in Kelsey's life.

When Kelsey's mind returned to the classroom, she heard people calling out their responses to the professor's question.

"He asks questions to show he's listening."

"She makes eye contact and comments on what I'm saying."

"Okay, I think we all get the picture," Professor Hartley responded. "To be as responsive as possible to your customers, listen carefully when they tell you what they need. If you have an unhappy customer, keep a positive attitude and remember that they need to be able to tell their story and feel heard. Either way, ask open-ended questions that will engage the customer in discussion. Pull information from them to gain a better understanding of their needs and their situation.

"As the customer shares information with you, acknowledge what they're saying through nonverbal communication—such as nodding your head—as well as verbal communication. Paraphrase what the customer just said—reflect their feelings so that they know you're actively listening. If they're unhappy, show empathy, or even apologize if it seems appropriate.

"After you think you have enough information and you know that the person feels they've been heard, offer to help them. Give the person a couple of options, if possible. The better you know your customer, the better you'll know the way to respond.

"Most unhappy customers just want the matter resolved. Keep in mind that the *situation*, not the customer, is the problem. Your job is to find a solution as quickly as possible—that's the key to leaving a positive impression. Statistics show that if you can kindly resolve their problem, 70 percent of unhappy customers will do business with you again. If you can kindly resolve their problem on the spot, 95 percent will do business with you again.

"When you take the time to listen to customers, you're showing them you care about them. Look them in the eye, smile, be sincere, and focus on the customers and their point of view. That's Responsiveness in action."

"Hi, Grandma Kate, I'm home," called Kelsey as she closed the front door behind her.

"I'm in here, honey," Grandma Kate called from the living room. "Come see what I got in the mail today."

As Kelsey walked into the room, her grandmother was holding up a card. "Can you believe that the people at the clinic sent me a birthday card? How on earth did they know my birthday was this week?"

"That's so nice," said Kelsey. "How *did* they know that?"

"I don't know, but it sure was a nice surprise," said Grandma Kate.

Kelsey quickly realized that Grandma Kate's date of birth was on file at the clinic. Still, it was definitely exceeding expectations for the clinic staff to send birthday cards to patients—a great example of how they put their Relationships value into action.

Because Steven had canceled their huddle on Monday, Kelsey was determined to get a few minutes with him on Wednesday to talk about the service initiative he was going to present to senior management. She'd put together a packet of everything she had studied in her course so far and had been putting a lot of thought into what Steven might want to say. It was just before lunch when she finally spotted him.

"Steven, would you have a few minutes today to talk about the service initiative presentation? I'd like to get your—"

"Kelsey," Steven interrupted, "I know we haven't had a chance to connect, and I'm really sorry, but today's not a good day. I'm going to be in meetings all afternoon. As a matter of fact," he said as he looked at his watch, "I'm running late right now. We'll have to touch base another time."

With that, he was gone. True to his word, he didn't appear for the rest of Kelsey's shift.

Kelsey left work feeling disappointed that another day had gone by with no progress. She wished she knew more about what was going on. All she knew was that morale at Ferguson's couldn't be lower.

Iris turned her attention to Grandma Kate as soon as she and Kelsey were settled in the therapy room at the clinic. Alex had joined them. "Before Alex gets started with your session today, I thought we'd spend a few minutes so that you can tell me how you're feeling about the progress we're making with your wrist," said Iris.

For the next 10 minutes or so, Iris asked questions and listened intently, even taking notes, as Grandma Kate answered them. Every now and then she would comment on something, but mostly she listened and Grandma Kate talked. Grandma Kate went into some detail about how her wrist felt today compared with the past few weeks and said she was sure the exercises she had been doing between sessions were helping her recovery. Iris listened patiently to her lament about how much she missed gardening, quilting, and other activities that needed both hands. Kelsey observed it all and thought, *Iris is showing more patience with Grandma Kate than I sometimes do.*

At the end of their talk, Iris said, "Well, Kate, based on what I've observed in the last few visits and what I just heard you say, I think you're definitely coming down the home stretch with your therapy. I'm going to modify your routine and see if we can get you out of that brace within the next week or two. Does that sound like a good plan to you?"

"That sounds wonderful," said Grandma Kate. "You know, I really appreciate your listening to my concerns. And I love how you never treat me like an old lady. I feel as if I'm your partner in getting my wrist back in working order."

"You're definitely our partner, especially since you're doing most of the work," said Alex with a smile.

"Listening to our patients is part of our job," said Iris. "If we don't know what they're thinking and feeling, we can't be effective in what we do." She stood up. "I'll leave you with Alex now, and he'll show you a few new exercises."

Kelsey decided to stay and watch their session today. She loved watching her grandma interact with both Alex and Iris.

They were so kind to her and made her laugh, even at times when the movements were uncomfortable for her. Alex had come to know Grandma Kate well enough that he would distract her from the less pleasant exercises by asking questions so that she would start talking. Kelsey thought her grandma might actually miss coming to these appointments after her wrist was healed.

When the session was over and they were on their way home, Grandma Kate said, "Iris and Alex have such a nice way about them. They want to know how I feel about things—and they take time to listen to me and make me feel special, as if I'm their only patient."

"This is what I'm learning about in my class right now—Responsiveness," said Kelsey. "Remember me telling you about the ICARE model? Iris and Alex are showing that they care about you. And you're healing ahead of schedule!"

"Why won't you tell me where we're going?" asked Grandma Kate. Kelsey had told her to be ready at nine o'clock Saturday morning, and they were now in the car, heading toward town.

"Because it's your birthday surprise," said Kelsey with a sneaky smile.

As Kelsey turned onto an unfamiliar street, Grandma Kate saw a large sign and exclaimed, "Oh, Kelsey. I haven't been to the zoo in years. What a wonderful birthday present."

"I bought tickets for the bus tour in advance, Grandma," Kelsey said. "That way we won't have to walk very far and we can see all the animals."

After they parked and entered the zoo, they made their way to the tour bus station. As they approached the large open-air bus, they were greeted by a jovial man with a handlebar mustache who held out his hand to Grandma Kate. He was wearing a uniform with a bow tie and a cap.

"Good morning, ladies. Allow me to assist you," he said. Grandma Kate took his hand, stepped up into the bus, and sat in the front seat next to the open window. Kelsey sat next to her grandma on the aisle. A middle-aged couple sat down across from them, directly behind the driver's seat.

The woman across from Kelsey said to her husband, "Ned, don't you think it would be nice to let me sit next to the window?"

The woman's husband immediately stood up and maneuvered his way past her so that she could slide over. He sat down in the aisle seat. More passengers boarded the bus until it was about half full.

"I don't understand why they don't make these seats more comfortable," the woman complained to her husband as the man with the mustache stepped up into the bus and sat in the driver's seat.

"This is going to be so much fun!" said Grandma Kate as she squeezed Kelsey's hand. Grandma Kate wasn't easy to shop for, so Kelsey was happy she'd chosen this for a birthday gift.

The driver pulled the bus out of the station and picked up his microphone to begin his tour guide spiel.

"Good morning, everyone! I hope you're all looking forward to a great day today here at the zoo. I've talked with all the animals this morning, and they've agreed to be on their best behavior and to pose for photo opportunities whenever we stop. The only one who was a little cranky about it was the musk ox, so I didn't argue with him," he chuckled. "You don't ever want to be on that guy's bad side!" Snickers and murmurs came from the passengers.

The woman sitting behind the bus driver leaned forward and said, "I hope you don't drive this fast all day. I feel like I'm going to get whiplash."

The bus driver turned off the microphone and said, "So sorry, ma'am; I'll watch my speed from now on. Most of the time I'll be going slowly so that everyone can take pictures. Sometimes in the morning I'm just eager to get to the animals so that you folks can start having fun. My apologies." He turned on the microphone and said, "We're getting close to the peacock and flamingo lagoon now, folks. I wonder if the peacock will put on a show for us. He told me he would."

Kelsey was impressed that the driver didn't seem to mind the woman's comment. As the tour went along, she noticed that he not only knew hundreds of details about the animals but also was able to answer everyone's questions. Throughout his interactions with the passengers, he kept a playful attitude and didn't miss a beat. *He really likes his job*, Kelsey thought.

Later in the tour, when the bus was stopped and Grandma Kate had turned away to take pictures of the giraffes and zebras, Kelsey leaned over and told the driver it was her grandmother's birthday. She had a hunch he might do something special for people's birthdays.

Sure enough, a few minutes later the bus stopped in front of the brown bear enclosure. The bear approached the front of the enclosure—a deep moat separating him from the road—and sat down as if he were posing for photos. The bus driver said, "This is our one-trick bear, Buster. Why do you all think I call him our 'one-trick bear'?

"Because he only has one trick!" some passengers called out. Everyone laughed.

The driver addressed the bear. "Hey, Buster—did you know there's a birthday girl on our bus? Her name is Kate." Grandma Kate gasped.

"Everybody, let's wave at Buster and see if we can get him to wave at Kate for her birthday. Hi, Buster!" The bus driver began to wave at the bear, and soon nearly everyone on the bus was waving. After a moment or two, Buster lifted his huge paw in the air and tossed his head. Kelsey and the other passengers snapped a picture at just the right moment.

Grandma Kate was delighted. "That was wonderful," she said to the driver. "Thank you for making my birthday special. How did you know?"

"A little bird told me," said the driver as he winked at Kelsey and put the bus in gear.

The remainder of the tour was just as enjoyable. When Kelsey got off the bus, she thanked the driver.

"How long have you been doing this job?" she asked.

As he held out his hand for the next passenger stepping off, the driver smiled and said, "I've been here 13 years as of last month. Best job I've ever had."

"I think people can tell you're having fun," said Kelsey. "You relate so well with your passengers—and you don't let the cranky ones get to you."

"Ha!" The driver laughed. "Well, you know, it's like I was saying about our old musk ox—sometimes it's best not to argue with someone. Listen to what they're really saying and try to meet their needs and stay on their good side. I just try to show people I care about them. It makes everyone's day better and helps keep the focus on the fun."

Just then, the woman who had been sitting behind the driver got off the bus, smiled at him, and said, "Thank you."

The driver smiled at the woman and said, "You're very welcome, ma'am." He raised his eyebrows and smiled at Kelsey.

Grandma Kate and Kelsey spent some time in the aviary and stopped by the petting zoo before they went home. It had been a wonderful day for both of them, and the tour guide's caring attitude had made a positive, lasting impression.

Monday was a long and challenging day at work for Kelsey. Not only did Steven not come in early for their huddle, but he canceled the regular Monday morning meeting altogether. He'd never done that before. Kelsey knew something big must be going on; she just didn't know what it was.

That afternoon, just before her shift was over, Kelsey saw her teammate Rob talking with a customer who was holding a large table lamp.

"I'm sorry, ma'am—we can't match prices from our competitors anymore," said Rob. "We just changed that policy. I'm very sorry."

"That's too bad," said the woman, frowning. "I really wanted a nice lamp like this for my office. Your price is $50, and Lamp World has one just like it for $40. I was hoping you could match their price so that I wouldn't have to drive all the way back there to get it, but I guess now I'll have to. I hate it when stores change their policies and don't tell customers about it." With some effort, she put the large lamp back on the shelf.

"I absolutely understand your frustration," Rob said in a sympathetic tone. He paused and said, "Lamp World—that's the big warehouse store across town, isn't it?"

"Yes. They have a huge selection—I'm sure that's why their prices are lower than yours," said the customer.

"If you don't mind my asking, ma'am—don't they price their lamps and lampshades separately?"

"Yes, they do, so that you can choose the combination you want," said the customer. "What are you getting at?"

"Were they asking $40 for the lamp *and* the shade, or just for the lamp?"

"Oh," said the customer, looking pensive. "Now that I think about it, I guess it was just for the lamp. Their shades are $20 extra. So I guess the total cost would've been $60."

Rob's face brightened as he gestured toward the lamp. "Our price on this lamp includes the shade. Do you like this combination?"

"Actually, I love this shade—it's very stylish." She smiled broadly. "So, in fact, I'm getting a *better* deal here at Ferguson's."

"Yes, you are," said Rob, lifting the lamp off the shelf. "If you're through with your shopping, I'll be happy to go through checkout with you and carry the lamp out to your car."

As the two walked away, Kelsey could hear the woman laughing and continuing to talk to Rob. Kelsey was impressed—not only with the way Rob had listened to his customer and solved the problem to her satisfaction but also with his knowledge of the other store's pricing policy. His attitude toward service had changed 180 degrees in just the last couple of months. Kelsey wondered if it could have had anything to do with the ideas she was passing along. *I've got to tell Steven about this so that he can mention it at the next Monday morning meeting*, Kelsey thought. *That's Responsiveness if I've ever seen it!*

By the time Kelsey and Grandma Kate got home from the clinic early that evening, Kelsey was so exhausted, all she wanted to do was eat dinner and go to bed. Unfortunately, she had a paper to write for class the next morning. After dinner, she forced herself to go to her room and study while Grandma Kate watched a movie in the living room.

Kelsey had just cracked open her textbook when her cell phone buzzed with a text. She didn't recognize the phone number, but the text read: *Hi Kelsey. This is Steven. Sorry to interrupt but do you have a few minutes to talk?*

Curious as to why her boss would need to call her on a Monday night, she texted back: *Sure.*

Within a minute, her phone rang.

"Hello?"

"Hi, Kelsey. I'm sorry to bother you."

"No worries; I was just studying. Is everything okay?"

"First, I want to apologize for being so short with you when we spoke last Wednesday. There's a lot of stuff going on right now. I had a meeting to get to, but I realized afterward that I'd cut you off in mid sentence. I feel bad we haven't had a chance to meet lately so that you could fill me in about what you're learning. I just want you to know I think you're a great employee and I really value having you in the department as part of our team."

At first, Kelsey didn't know what to say—she was surprised to hear Steven apologize.

"Thanks, Steven. I really appreciate your calling. I know things are crazy in the store right now, but when you have time, I've got some more information to share with you that we can use to build the service initiative. In fact, we can talk about it right now if you want to." She tapped her laptop and opened the folder containing her notes from class.

"That's the other reason I'm calling you," he said. "I guess there's no other way to say this—I can't ask you to spend any more time on this plan. There isn't any point. I spoke with the store manager today and told him you and I were putting together a customer service initiative. He shut me down and said right now, all they can focus on is increasing revenue and cutting costs. They just don't understand the importance of creating customer loyalty; it's all about the numbers to them."

Kelsey was quiet on the other end, taking in what Steven had said.

"I can't tell you how disappointed I am about this, Kelsey—especially with all the thought and effort you've been putting into it."

"That makes two of us," said Kelsey.

"Anyway, I hope you don't let this get you down too much. You know I still appreciate your enthusiasm and your good ideas—and I want you to keep sharing your suggestions with the team and me, so that at least our department can shine in spite of everything else that's going on. Things are bound to calm down, and when they do, maybe we can try again."

"Well, thanks for believing in me, Steven," said Kelsey sadly. "I guess we'll just keep doing the best we can in our department and see what happens."

Kelsey was so disturbed by Steven's news that it took her a while to open her book after she put down the phone. She appreciated his calling and apologizing, though—he really was a nice man and a good manager. *He deserves better than this—*

and maybe I do, too, she thought. *How ironic that I'm studying about the benefits of being a good listener and none of the leaders at my store want to listen to common sense.* She and Steven both knew Ferguson's was going down the wrong path, but nobody who was in a position to do anything about it seemed to care.

She forced herself to finish her paper and then jotted down some thoughts about a new plan that was forming in her head. She was going to call Iris in the morning to see when they could meet—she needed an outsider's perspective.

9

Empowerment

Kelsey arrived and took her seat just as Professor Hartley was walking to the front of the room.

"Good morning, everybody. Let's start with a pop quiz on what we've learned so far." Professor Hartley loved giving pop quizzes for review, and he made them fun. Kelsey had been remembering everything so well and getting so much out of the class, she almost felt as if she could teach it.

When the quiz was over, the professor opened his laptop. "Are you ready for the final letter in ICARE?" he asked. He tapped his keyboard and the screen read:

> **I – Ideal Service**
>
> **C – Culture of Service**
>
> **A – Attentiveness**
>
> **R – Responsiveness**
>
> **E – Empowerment**

"You have complete control over some things on your job. For instance, you can find out more about a product on your own, you can be more attentive to your customers, and you always have control over your own performance. There are other parts of your job that you can't directly control but may be able to influence. Examples of these would be your authority to make decisions, whether your manager trusts you, or whether your manager will listen if you offer feedback. All these things come under the category of *Empowerment*."

He tapped the keyboard again and revealed the next slide.

> **Empowerment:**
> Taking the initiative
> to implement the service vision.

"So let's discuss this. What makes you feel empowered on your job? Just call out whatever comes to mind," prompted the professor.

From around the room, students offered examples.

"When I don't have to ask for help to do something."

"When my boss listens to an idea I have."

"When I'm asked for my opinion."

"When I can solve a customer's problem on my own."

"When I know more about a product than my coworkers do."

"Good answers," said the professor. "Now can you think of something you've done on your own—something to empower *yourself* on the job? Josie, you have your hand up."

"I asked my boss if the company could pay for me to take a course on a new computer program I could use on my job, and it was approved. Now I can respond to inquiries a lot faster," said Josie.

"Connor, what about you?"

"A few weeks ago, I decided to learn the names of the customers who come to my window at the bank, even though we don't have to. I notice those people choosing my line now, on purpose," said Connor.

"Great examples!" said the professor. "The more empowered the frontline people in an organization are, the happier the external customers are going to be, because their needs are being met. Having empowered employees ultimately will benefit the customer."

As students continued sharing their examples, Kelsey thought about how excited she'd been about improving customer service at Ferguson's over the last couple of months. She had tried to empower herself by bringing her ideas to work, but her suggestions never got any further than her department manager. She was so discouraged that she felt as if she didn't have control over *any* part of her job anymore.

Toward the end of class, Professor Hartley announced, "Empowerment is an integral part of the ICARE model, so we're going to talk more about it next week. In the meantime, here's your assignment: make a list of the parts of your job where you're empowered and how you got there—was it already part of your organization's culture, or did you make it happen yourself? Then think about areas where you're not in control but would like to be more empowered. Write two or three pages on each and go into as much detail as you can."

The students stood up and began to move toward the door as the professor called out, "Oh—and don't forget to go into the online class portal and read the articles I posted. You never know when I may be in the mood for another pop quiz!"

Kelsey stayed after class to talk to Professor Hartley about the phone conversation she'd had with Steven.

"I think you should keep working on your plan," said the professor. "If your company isn't open to it, you'll eventually be able to propose it somewhere else. You know, Kelsey, Ferguson's isn't the only place in town. If they don't want to change, perhaps you need to find a place that's a better values match for you."

Kelsey thanked him for his understanding and walked toward the door.

"I'd still be more than happy to talk to Dan for you if you'd like," the professor called out.

Kelsey looked back and smiled. "Thanks, Professor. I'm thinking about taking you up on that offer. I'll let you know soon."

All Kelsey could think about was what it would be like to work somewhere else. Maybe changing jobs really would be her best move.

Eager to get feedback from her mentor and friend, Kelsey had arranged to meet Iris at the clinic early that evening after Iris's last therapy appointment.

Iris's office was warm and casual—just as she was. As Kelsey walked in, Iris rose from behind her desk and came around to sit in a chair beside the one she offered to Kelsey.

"You sounded pretty dejected on the phone this morning, Kelsey. Tell me what's going on."

Kelsey unloaded about the strange and stressful atmosphere at work, her disappointment at senior management's rejecting the idea of a customer service initiative, and what Professor Hartley had said about talking to Mr. Murray for her.

"So," she finished with a sigh, "I'm thinking about applying to work at ShopSmart. What do you think?"

"What do *you* think?" asked Iris.

"After learning about the importance of caring for customers and how to build a business around a Culture of Service, I'm convinced that Ferguson's just isn't focused on the right things. I also get nervous thinking about the impact ShopSmart may have on our store and that I could even be out of a job if things don't go well."

"That's not a good feeling."

"No, it's not—and I know I'm really trying my best to help things get better. But the senior leaders aren't interested in what I have to say. What do I know? I'm just an hourly employee." Kelsey could feel her frustration growing again just talking about it.

"I think you should go for it, Kelsey," Iris said firmly. "You're a positive person, you're very conscientious about your job, and you really care about your customers. With your service mindset, I think ShopSmart would see you as a perfect addition to its team. It makes sense that you'd probably move up faster there, too, since you already share their service vision. And you wouldn't feel as if you were pounding your head against the wall anymore—you'd actually feel appreciated."

"But what if I don't get the job?"

"You wouldn't be any worse off than you are now. Apply and see what happens. This is your career you're talking about. Believe in yourself. I know they'd be lucky to have someone like you!"

Iris's words were exactly what Kelsey needed to hear. She felt a rush of resilience. "You're right—I've got nothing to lose. I'm going to apply tomorrow." Kelsey was relieved to have finally made the decision. "Thanks for listening, Iris. You're a wonderful person to have in my corner. This is all about empowerment—taking control of my own life instead of waiting for something to happen."

As she considered her fresh decision on the way home, Kelsey felt a pang of guilt—almost as if she were abandoning Steven. *I'll just tell him up front that I'm applying at ShopSmart,* she thought. *Maybe he'll think about moving over there, too!*

Kelsey got up early the next morning so that she could fill out an online application for ShopSmart before she got ready for work. There was a place to sign up for a face-to-face interview, so she scheduled an appointment for Friday morning—her day off.

She moved her cursor to the *Submit* square on her laptop screen.

"Submit!" she said out loud as she tapped her laptop. There—she'd done it!

As she was dressing for work, she experienced another twinge of anxiety. But she told herself she wasn't quitting her job—just keeping her options open.

When Kelsey arrived at the store, everyone was acting uneasy again. She heard some new rumors that changes were coming in the next few days, but of course nobody knew any details.

I wonder who they're laying off now, Kelsey thought. She caught herself and decided she had to stop thinking so negatively. *This is what Mr. Murray was talking about. I'm not even giving my company a fighting chance anymore. I've become jaded—and that's not like me.*

It was hard for Kelsey to concentrate on her work, but she did her best. To her surprise, as the day went by, she found herself noticing a few small, positive changes. Maybe it was because of the rumors, but she witnessed some floor managers stepping in to help with long lines and talking to customers. She also saw a couple of new people working—could Ferguson's be hiring again?

Kelsey would have asked Steven about it, but she didn't see him all day. She decided to leave him a voice mail and ask for some time to talk the next morning. She had to let him know she was going to interview at ShopSmart on Friday. It was the least she could do, since he'd been so supportive of her, especially in the past several weeks.

On their way to the clinic, Kelsey talked with Grandma Kate about having applied at ShopSmart that morning—and about the second thoughts that were beginning to creep in.

"This morning when I submitted my application, I was sure I was doing the right thing—but now I don't know if I'm really ready to give up on Ferguson's. Today I saw some signs that our store management might be starting to care more about the employees and the customers."

"There's something to be said for being loyal to your company, honey—but make sure you're also being true to yourself," said Grandma Kate. "This is your future, and these are your career opportunities. If you're convinced that you've come to a dead end where you are, there's nothing wrong with making a change."

"You're right," said Kelsey, feeling confident again about her decision.

Grandma Kate looked thoughtful. "At the same time, though, think hard about whether you've done everything you can to influence people at your store. The grass isn't always greener on the other side, you know."

Kelsey sighed. *Great. Now I'm just as confused as before.*

When they walked in the door, Alex was standing at the receptionist's desk. "Hello, Mrs. Wilson," he said cheerfully. "Have you been doing your home therapy exercises so that we can start seeing less of you?"

"I sure have," said Grandma Kate. "When you told me I was almost finished with this darn brace, I promised myself I was going to follow your instructions to the letter. As a matter of fact, I think my wrist is almost back to normal."

After Alex took Grandma Kate back to the therapy room for their session, Kelsey sat down in the waiting area and picked up a magazine. A woman who looked to be in her thirties was sitting nearby and leaned toward Kelsey.

"I'm waiting for my dad," the woman said. "He's got back problems."

"Oh, that's too bad," said Kelsey. "I'm with my grandmother—I drive her to her appointments."

"Do you work?" asked the woman. "Sorry—I know that's kind of a nosy question, but I'm unemployed, and I've discovered that networking in waiting rooms sometimes can be a good way to find out who's hiring," she said.

Kelsey smiled. "Yes—I work at Ferguson's."

The woman shook her head and groaned. "Ugh. I worked in retail last year. Hated it. I could never tell what the customers wanted, and the managers were always yelling at me and telling me what to do." She flipped a page in her magazine and continued. "After about six months, I got fed up and switched to a different store because I heard that it paid more. But once I got there, I found out everybody in that store hated each other, and they were all really lazy. I was the best employee there, but my manager didn't hold anybody accountable, so I always ended up doing everybody else's work. I left that place without even giving notice. Then I wished I hadn't quit the first job, but they'd filled my position right away. I'm still looking for work."

As the woman spoke, Kelsey could feel her anxiety growing once again. She thought about calling and canceling her interview with ShopSmart until she was more certain about what she should do.

Then, just as quickly, her rational side regained control. *My situation is nothing like hers*, she thought. She simply had to find Steven first thing in the morning and talk to him. She felt secure enough in her relationship with him to take the chance.

Even though Steven hadn't responded to her message, Kelsey purposely got to work 30 minutes early on Thursday in the hope of catching him before the store opened. She found him in the break room pouring himself a cup of coffee.

"Hi, Steven—I was hoping to talk to you before everyone got here. Do you have a few minutes?"

"Sure. I got your message. I want to talk to you, too." They sat down across from each other at the break table.

"Well—" She hesitated, wondering for a moment whether this was a good idea. *Just say it, Kelsey!* "I'm thinking about applying for a job over at ShopSmart." She took a deep breath, and the words came pouring out. "In fact, I've already applied there—and I have an appointment for an interview tomorrow. I really like working with you, Steven. You've been such a good boss, and I know you're really trying to make things better around here—but I don't think this company is a good fit for me anymore." *Phew. Done.*

Steven didn't say anything for a few seconds. When he spoke again, his tone was quiet and sincere.

"Believe me, Kelsey, I completely understand why you think Ferguson's isn't a good match for you any longer. Actually, I'd been feeling the same way until very recently. I don't blame you at all for applying at ShopSmart. I also considered going there, but I decided against it—and I hope you will, too." He paused again, and Kelsey got the impression he was weighing his words carefully.

"Okay. This isn't public knowledge yet, so you have to keep it to yourself. It's going to be announced within the next few days," said Steven in a low voice, looking at the door. Kelsey leaned in.

"With our numbers going down and customer complaints going up in the past year, some major changes have just happened at the corporate level. They've replaced the CEO. And even though I can't give you any details, I can tell you that the new person will be totally committed to both our employees and our customers. Ferguson's is going to be a top-notch retail organization, Kelsey—somewhere we're all going to be proud to work."

Kelsey was speechless. This explained why the mood around the store had seemed so strange.

He continued. "Do you want to know why I wasn't here yesterday?"

Kelsey nodded her head and stared at him, concentrating on what he was saying.

"I was called in to meet the new CEO. I didn't know why they were calling me in—I even thought, with all of the weird stuff going on, maybe I was going to get fired. But it turned out the CEO wanted to meet and talk with me because Home and Office is the only department in our store that isn't floundering. Our department has customers praising our service, not complaining about it. And Kelsey—you've been a big part of that success. Because of your strong beliefs about service and your great role modeling, you've made everyone on our team want to do a better job."

"Oh, wow," was all Kelsey could say.

"At the end of our conversation, the new CEO offered me the job of store manager, here at this store. The company wants us to be the flagship store for the new customer-focused culture they're going to create companywide."

Kelsey gasped, "Oh, Steven! That's just great!" and began to stand up. She was so happy for Steven, she wanted to hug him.

"Hold on, sit down for a second," Steven said with a laugh. "There's more." Kelsey sat down.

"So—here's the thing. I've been cleared by HR to offer you *my* job—department manager for Home and Office—but I was supposed to wait until the news came out about the new CEO and my promotion. But now, with you saying you're going to interview at ShopSmart tomorrow, I don't want to risk losing you to them. So I'm offering it to you right now, Kelsey. I really want you on the team. Please—think about it."

Her head reeling, Kelsey quickly found her voice. "Steven, I can't believe this. I don't know what to say. Everyone's been talking about layoffs, and I was worried about what would happen to us when ShopSmart opened and whether I might lose my job—and here you are telling me the exact opposite!"

Steven relaxed as he spoke. "With everything that's gone on around the store in the last few months, morale has been terrible, and people have been assuming the worst. I'm positive that with the new, stronger leadership and teamwork, we can turn that perception around and make our store a great place to work."

"Ferguson's is so lucky to have you as store manager—you'll be great! Congratulations."

"Thanks—but you haven't said anything about whether you're interested in the department manager position."

"I'm really flattered, Steven, but I don't know if I'm ready to be a manager," said Kelsey.

"Kelsey, think about the last couple of months and how you've been the one coming to me with suggestions and ideas on how to improve what we do around here. You really *care*. And because of your desire to serve our customers and make this department successful, I caught the eye of the new CEO! You made me look good. I'd be crazy *not* to promote you."

Kelsey smiled. "Thanks, Steven. That's nice of you to say."

"We need all our people to understand the importance of true customer service. So, to that end, we want to establish a Legendary Service Culture team at each location. These teams will be focused on creating and sustaining our Culture of Service. The new CEO wants the first team to be launched here at our store—so in addition to leading our Home and Office Department team, Kelsey, you'd be heading up that first Legendary Service Culture team and teaching them what you've been teaching me. It's a huge responsibility, but I'll be right here to help you and support what you're doing. After we get our team in place, we'll probably want you to go to our other stores as they set up their own teams so that you can train all the team leaders."

Kelsey couldn't believe it. This was exactly the kind of thing she'd had in mind when she started coming to Steven with the ideas from her class—and now, with the blessing of the new CEO, it was actually happening!

She could hardly contain her excitement. "Steven, I don't have to think about it anymore. I would be honored to be part of the management team here. We're going to make Ferguson's a store where people want to work and customers want to shop."

"Yes! I can't tell you how happy I am to hear you say that. Welcome to the team! Maybe I'll start calling you Professor Young," said Steven with a big grin as he came around the table and shook Kelsey's hand enthusiastically. Then he looked toward the door and said quietly, "Now here's the hard part: you absolutely *have* to keep this to yourself until the announcement is made to the rest of the staff. It might take a few days. Corporate needs to tie up some loose ends before they can announce the new CEO to everyone."

"Is it okay if I tell my family?"

Steven winced. "If you're really careful—but only your immediate family, please. The news will be out soon enough. We don't want to steal the headlines."

Just then, the door opened as people began arriving for work. Steven and Kelsey smiled at each other as she turned and left the room.

When Kelsey took her lunch break later in the day, she noticed signs in the break room announcing a special all-company meeting on Monday morning at seven-thirty. Attendance was mandatory. Monday! Could she keep this quiet until *Monday*?

Kelsey spent the rest of her workday hoping that her face wasn't giving her away. She couldn't stop smiling as she thought about this strange twist of fate. She had finally convinced herself she was ready to interview at ShopSmart—and now, instead, she was going to be the manager of her department! *My Empowerment assignment for Professor Hartley will be a piece of cake now*, she thought. She couldn't wait for Tuesday's class—she would have a lot to share!

Kelsey burst through the front door and ran to the kitchen phone as she called out to her grandmother. "Grandma Kate, you're never going to believe what happened today! Come here and listen to the phone call I'm going to make!"

Grandma Kate came hurrying around the corner. "What's going on? It must be something awfully good."

Kelsey studied a number she'd written on a sticky note as she punched buttons on the phone.

"Hello? Yes. My name is Kelsey Young, and I have an appointment for a job interview with HR tomorrow morning at ten o'clock. Yes, I'll hold."

With a twinkle in her eye, Kelsey looked across the room at Grandma Kate and held up her finger. She mouthed the word *wait.*

"Yes? Yes, Kelsey Young, ten o'clock. I just need to let you know I have to cancel my interview. No—not reschedule, just cancel. Why?" She smiled broadly. "Well—I guess you could say I changed my mind. Okay. Thank you, too. Goodbye." She hung up the phone and pumped her fists in the air triumphantly as she grinned at her grandmother.

"Kelsey Young, tell me right now what you're up to!" Grandma Kate insisted.

"You are looking at the new *manager* of the Home and Office Department at Ferguson's!"

"Oh, my goodness! I'm so happy for you, honey!" Grandma Kate exclaimed as she held out her arms and they met in the center of the kitchen for a bear hug.

Noticing that something was different, Kelsey pulled away and said, "Grandma, why aren't you wearing your wrist brace?"

"Well, that's *my* news of the day, although it's not nearly as exciting as yours," Grandma Kate said with a smile. "Iris called today and told me I didn't need to wear the brace anymore as long as I kept up with my new exercises."

"That's wonderful," said Kelsey.

Grandma Kate continued. "After my session with Alex yesterday, he told Iris he felt that my wrist had healed to the point where I could start going without the brace—and he thinks I need only one or two more sessions at the clinic. Isn't it nice that Iris could go by Alex's recommendation instead of having to examine me herself?"

"Grandma, that's a great example of Empowerment, the last part of the ICARE model—we learned about it in class this week," said Kelsey.

"Oh, you and your ICARE model," said Grandma Kate with a laugh and a wave of her hand.

"Don't laugh—the ICARE model represents the five biggest reasons I've been promoted to department manager!" Kelsey danced a few steps around the kitchen floor.

"This calls for ice cream for dinner!" exclaimed Grandma Kate. "You get the bowls and scoop, I'll get the chocolate brownie chunk, and you can tell me everything."

The energy at Ferguson's on Monday morning was electrifying. The employees had heard that good news, not bad, was going to be announced, so everyone was gathered at the front of the store, eager to find out what was going on. At exactly seven-thirty, a woman Kelsey had never seen before came to the podium at the front of the room and called everyone to attention.

"Good morning! Thanks so much for coming in early today. By the way, in case you're wondering, you *will* be paid for attending this meeting."

Cheers rose from the group, followed by low murmuring.

"Most of you don't know me, but my name is Gretchen Holden and I'm chairman of Ferguson's board of directors. I'm sure that by now, many of you have heard about changes being made in the organization. Over the last year, we have come to the conclusion that the numbers on financial reports aren't the only thing that makes an organization successful. Through employee surveys, we found out our internal customers—that means all of you—weren't feeling valued for your contributions."

Suddenly, you could have heard a pin drop.

"What's more, customer surveys told us our external customers weren't feeling valued, either. Both of these findings were completely unacceptable—and we came to realize that our organization was going to have to make some very big changes if we wanted to stay in business. Ferguson's had a critical need for a companywide Culture of Service initiative—and the change needed to start at the top.

"We held many executive meetings regarding this proposal. A few leaders didn't share the vision and couldn't see themselves getting on board with it. They thought everything was fine the way it was and didn't see the need for a change. Those people are no longer with the organization."

Audible gasps could be heard in the crowd.

"We are confident that the leaders who remain, along with the newly hired members of our executive leadership team, are going to take Ferguson's to new heights of service—and financial success. We're all very excited about the possibilities that lie ahead, and we want you to know we are committed to you—our people. You're the ones who make it all possible."

She paused as the crowd applauded.

"With that, I'd like to introduce our new chief executive officer. He comes to us with an abundance of experience in the industry, most recently as vice president of operations for ShopSmart. Please join me in welcoming Mr. Dan Murray."

Everyone started applauding and strained to get a glimpse of the new CEO as he made his way to the podium. Kelsey couldn't believe her ears—or her eyes—when she saw the chairman hand the microphone to Dan Murray.

"Thank you, Gretchen. I want to start by letting all of you know how happy I am to be part of this great organization. I look forward to meeting each of you while I'm here over the next few days. We're going to make this location the flagship store for our new service culture initiative, particularly since ShopSmart will be our neighbor soon—and I know exactly how good *they* are," he said with a twinkle in his eye.

"Now I'd like to introduce someone who is no stranger to you. This person has stood out as a true leader in your store and is motivated to help develop the next generation of managers at Ferguson's. Please join me in congratulating your new store manager, Mr. Steven Walker."

Through cheers and applause, Steven made his way to the front and shook hands with Dan. Kelsey thought he looked a little self-conscious, but he was smiling as he took the microphone.

"I want to thank the board and Mr. Murray for giving me this fantastic opportunity. I look forward to working with all of you and hearing your ideas for how we can join together to make our store the employer of choice for our people, the store of choice for our customers, and a profitable, well-run organization for our owners." He pumped his fist in the air. "And I'm ready for us to *take on ShopSmart!*" he said to a loud ovation.

When the meeting was over and everyone had dispersed, Steven arrived in the Home and Office Department and called a quick team huddle.

"I want you all to know that I wouldn't have received this promotion if it hadn't been for each of you doing your best to make our department stand out. Thank you so much for your hard work these past few months, especially when changes were happening and you didn't know what was going on. I'm going to be in a dual role for the next several weeks as I make the transition from department manager to store manager, but I'll be here and available whenever you need me."

He turned and gestured toward Kelsey. "I'm happy to announce that Kelsey Young will be taking my place as manager of Home and Office."

Everyone congratulated Kelsey with smiles, hugs, and words of support.

Later, as Kelsey was about to leave for lunch, Steven and Dan Murray walked up.

"Kelsey, I was happy to hear from Steven that you've agreed to be the new manager of this department. Congratulations," said Dan as he shook Kelsey's hand.

"Thanks, Mr. Murray," said Kelsey with a smile. "I was so shocked when you walked up to the microphone! After hearing the things you said to my class a few weeks ago, I know how lucky we are to have you."

"Remember—it's Dan," he said. "When I spoke to your class, I was in negotiations with Ferguson's, but of course I couldn't say anything about it because nothing was final yet. ShopSmart is a great organization, and I'm extremely proud of what we accomplished there, but I was ready for a new challenge. Now we have a great opportunity to work together and make Ferguson's a service leader, starting with this store. I'm glad to have you on the team, Kelsey. I know you're going to help us make the changes necessary to implement our vision."

"I can't wait to apply all the great methods I've been learning in Professor Hartley's course," said Kelsey. "I'm very excited to be part of the management team."

Dan made his way around to talk to everyone in the department and then moved on to meet people in other departments.

Before Steven walked away, he said, "Kelsey, let's set aside some time next week to discuss your transition as well as things we can do to start creating a real service mindset here."

Kelsey sighed happily as she watched Steven walk away. Everything was finally falling into place.

The rest of the day flew by. Kelsey had a million ideas running through her head for things she wanted to accomplish within her department and also on the Legendary Service Culture team. Relieved that she no longer had to keep her promotion a secret, she spent some time that night texting friends—and tomorrow she would be able to give the news to Professor Hartley and the rest of the class.

"Good morning, everyone. We have a full day, so let's get started," said Professor Hartley.

"Last week I asked you to think about situations where you feel empowered in your job. Anyone want to offer an example?"

Kelsey's hand shot up.

"Since starting this course and learning so much about customer service, I've been making suggestions at work to see if Ferguson's could apply some of the methods we've been learning. My department manager, Steven, really liked the idea of improving our service and seemed to appreciate my interest. But other than Steven, it seemed as if nobody cared. The more I looked around, the more I could see that we weren't going to be able to impact customers the way we wanted to, and I got discouraged. Then, when Dan Murray came to speak to our class, I realized ShopSmart had the culture I was looking for. That's when I started thinking about working there.

"But last Thursday, the day before I was going to interview at ShopSmart, everything changed. I learned that Ferguson's was going to get a new CEO—and it turned out to be Mr. Murray! Steven got promoted to store manager and asked me to take his place as the Home and Office Department manager. He also wants me to help set up Legendary Service Culture teams at all of our stores. He said he chose me because I had shown interest in improving the service culture at our store, and he could tell I really cared about our internal and external customers."

"Well, that's a pretty exciting turn of events," said the professor. "Congratulations!"

"I really want to thank you, Professor Hartley, for talking about the importance of relationships and the different ways of caring for customers," said Kelsey. "I know that made all the difference."

"That's a great example of Empowerment in action— taking control of things that affect you. I know you'll enjoy working with Dan. You'll learn a lot from him. He's a great guy," said the professor.

"Now I'd like everyone to take 10 minutes to find a partner and share a story about a time during this past week when you felt empowered on your job."

The room buzzed for several minutes. Then the professor held up his hand and said, "Who just heard a good story from their partner that they want to share with the class?"

A young woman raised her hand.

"Mariana, I see you were talking with Nathan. What's his Empowerment story?"

"Nathan really likes his job at the country club," began Mariana, "but he hasn't had a raise in two years. Last week, after we talked about Empowerment in class, he made an appointment to meet with his supervisor. When he went to the meeting, he gave his boss a paper that listed his personal qualities, skills, and accomplishments, as well as ways that he felt his job performance had improved. He also brought notes he'd saved from two of the club members, praising him for going the extra mile to provide good service. Nathan said that during the meeting he focused on being polite and professional, and on asking for what he needed. His boss told him that he was impressed with his initiative and gave him a two-dollar-an-hour raise."

"Thanks, Mariana—that's a perfect example of Empowerment. And Nathan—congratulations on the raise!" The professor looked around the room. "Who else has a story to share?"

Several hands went up this time.

"Hank, you had Mason as a partner. What's his story?"

"Well, Mason works on the phone at one of those big call centers where they take complaints and do troubleshooting all day long. He said sometimes the stress kind of gets to him and his buddies. So about a year ago, he and some other people started talking to their HR department about getting some kind of a stress-busting area fixed up where they could go during their breaks and lunch. HR already had a wellness program, so they were interested in hearing the ideas. It's been in the works for a while, and last week, they finally opened a big new employee lounge with picnic tables, vending machines, a cabinet full of board games, a Ping-Pong table, and—" He turned to Mason. "What was that other thing, Mason?"

"Air hockey. We even have air hockey!" said Mason with a smile.

"There's a company that cares about its people," said Professor Hartley.

After a few more students shared stories, he asked, "Okay, class, what common themes are we hearing in these stories?"

"People took the initiative to affect their own future—they didn't wait for someone else to do it for them," one student commented.

Another student said, "It was like they were in control. They figured out what they wanted and found a way to make it happen."

"Exactly," said Professor Hartley. "Remember the Empowerment strategy about being in control of things that affect you? You need to take control of things that are important to you and take the lead to make them happen. An added benefit, as I've touched on before, is that people who are treated well at work will pass along that respect and good-will to their customers. As a result, customers will be more loyal to that organization and maybe even tell their friends about how they were treated. When they do that, they essentially become part of the company's sales force. When people feel valued for their contributions and are empowered to make decisions, they're more passionate about their job and their organization. That has a direct impact on customers—as well as on the ever-important bottom line.

"Now," said the professor, "what happens when you *don't* take control of things that are important to you?"

"You end up always doing what someone else wants you to do—but that might not be what you want for yourself or what's best for your coworkers or your customers," a student said.

"And whose fault is that?" the professor asked hypothetically. "Too many times, people play the victim at work, thinking that their managers should know what they need— as if managers were able to read minds. Talking to your supervisor about what you need is part of Empowerment. It's great when managers are in tune with their employees, but you can't expect them to know all of your needs or interests unless you tell them. And if managers don't know what their people need, in the end, it could be bad for the organization. This also applies to asking your supervisor for feedback on whether you're doing a good job. You don't necessarily have to wait a year for your annual performance review—ask for a one-on-one meeting to get specifics on what you're doing right and where you need to improve."

The professor went on. "Since frontline employees are closest to the customer, it's critical for an organization, on a day-to-day basis, to have a way of capturing the information frontline folks hear from customers as a way to improve service. The best organizations ask employees to pass feedback, good and bad, up the ladder so that leaders can decide whether they need to take action. This simple process can be essential for a company's success."

"Now I have good news and bad news," said the professor. "The good news is that once leaders and employees have learned the ICARE model, they have the knowledge and skills they need to start putting the model into action. The bad news is that most companies stop right there and don't put a sustainability plan in place to make sure people are using these new skills. Someone in the organization—preferably a team—needs to be appointed to keep service on everyone's mind."

Kelsey felt a surge of excitement as she thought about the Legendary Service Culture team she would be heading up at Ferguson's.

"The challenge with any kind of training, especially when an organization is trying to change its culture," said the professor, "is that the learning needs to stay at the front of everyone's mind. If this doesn't happen, and if new behaviors aren't praised and old behaviors redirected, it's very easy for employees to return to their old ways.

"It all goes back to what I said on the first day of class—it starts with relationships. If we can all work on creating and sustaining a culture of nurturing the relationships we have with one another and with our external customers, our organizations can't help but reap the benefits."

What a different attitude I have when I feel good about my job, Kelsey thought as she drove to work Monday morning.

Although she wouldn't officially take over as department manager for another month, she felt compelled to get to the morning meeting before everyone else did to set a good example and to greet her coworkers and make them feel welcome. *It's all about relationships and building a strong team,* she thought as people started walking in.

After the meeting, Steven and Kelsey met in Steven's office. Even though Steven was now the store manager, he was also continuing as the department manager until Kelsey could be trained properly. They spent an hour talking about Kelsey's upcoming transition.

"I want to make sure we set you up for success in this position, Kelsey," said Steven. "Managing people is a lot different from being an individual contributor, and believe me, I still have plenty to learn about leadership. I'm looking forward to working with you to make this store the best it can be." He gave her a schedule of ongoing training for the next few months, including an online module that would help her develop her leadership skills.

"Now," he said as he leaned back in his chair, "let me hear your ideas for the Legendary Service Culture team. I know you've probably been thinking about it every day since you learned it would be part of your new job."

Kelsey laughed. "Yes, actually, I have," she said, getting out her notes. "Tell me what you think of these ideas. Each store's LSC team will have a representative from each department who is responsible for going to the weekly LSC team meetings and taking information back to their department manager. The department manager would follow through with the Legendary Service and ICARE model training for associates during their weekly department meetings.

"The other half of each LSC team member's role would be to come to meetings ready to report their department's progress on putting the new service vision into practice. They would also pass along any feedback their department receives from customers about our new Culture of Service—hopefully, positive confirmation that our new culture was affecting customers in a good way."

"So far it all sounds great—tell me more," said Steven, obviously pleased.

"Since we're beta testing the LSC team concept first at our store, I'd like to send a memo to our department managers today or tomorrow," continued Kelsey, "to ask each of them to appoint an associate to serve a three-month term on the LSC team. And I think it would be good for each store to compensate the LSC team members with a Ferguson's gift card at the end of their term, as a way of thanking them for serving on the team."

"We'll work through the details, but you're definitely covering all the bases. I knew you'd be the right person to head this up," said Steven. "Between your new manager duties and setting up the LSC teams, you're going to be a very busy woman for a few months!"

Kelsey left work that day tired but content. She was finally part of an organization that really cared about people.

10

Six Months
Later

Six months after the leadership change at Ferguson's, every store had the company's service vision and values posted in the store entry for all to see:

> **Ferguson's Service Vision**
>
> To Provide Genuine Value
> and Caring Service
> to Every Customer, Every Day

Ferguson's Values

Ethical Behavior

Do the right thing

Relationships

Build mutual trust and respect with
customers, colleagues, and community

Success

Run a profitable business

Learning

Continuously improve—
as individuals and as an organization

Kelsey felt privileged to have Steven and Dan as mentors to teach her the basics of leadership. It helped that she already shared their belief that if an organization's leaders take care of their people, their people will take care of the customers, and the customers will come back—resulting in a successful organization.

When word got around that the man who had made ShopSmart number one in customer service was now CEO of Ferguson's, customers began coming in to see what was different. Ferguson's numbers began to improve immediately. Dan's office was inundated with complimentary letters and e-mails praising the changes and the renewed emphasis on service. Kelsey's store held its own against the new ShopSmart store in the first quarter it was open, and Ferguson's market share actually surpassed that of ShopSmart in the second quarter.

The Legendary Service Culture teams were up and running in all Ferguson's locations. Kelsey and Steven, with the help of the LSC team members, had come up with several entertaining, hands-on activities to help train employees in the ICARE model, which made the LSC meetings fun. As a result, each department manager now had to choose among many willing volunteers when it came time to appoint an LSC team member for each new three-month term.

Kelsey's department meeting with her Home and Office team fell exactly on the six-month anniversary of her new position. Toward the end of the meeting, everyone was surprised when there was a knock on the door and Dan and Steven walked in.

Kelsey turned toward them and smiled. "Hello! What a nice surprise."

Steven held the door open, and Grandma Kate appeared behind him, beaming from ear to ear.

"Oh, my gosh," exclaimed Kelsey. "Grandma Kate! What are you doing here?"

"You'll find out in a minute," said Grandma Kate with a sly smile.

"May I have the floor?" Steven asked.

"Of course!"

Steven turned to the group as Dan and Grandma Kate stood to the side. "In honor of her first six months of service to our store in her dual role as Home and Office Department manager and Legendary Service Culture team trainer, I have the privilege of expressing our appreciation to Kelsey Young for her tireless devotion to Ferguson's new service vision." He turned to Kelsey and said, "Kelsey, you are truly making a difference in our organization." He handed her an envelope along with a plaque and read the plaque's inscription out loud to the group:

> **Kelsey Young**
> Ferguson's Legendary Service
> Culture Champion Extraordinaire

The Home and Office team stood up and applauded. They knew how hard Kelsey had been working and how well she treated everyone, and they were happy to see her receive this recognition.

After the presentation, Steven, Dan, and Grandma Kate stayed while Kelsey brought the meeting to a close. When the associates had all left, Kelsey said, "Dan and Steven, thank you so much for this. I don't know what to say."

"I know we still have a lot to accomplish," said Steven, "but we wanted to celebrate your efforts up to this point—

and to let you know how much we appreciate you and what you do."

"You've got a great future with us, Kelsey," said Dan with a smile.

"I'm so proud of you, honey," said Grandma Kate.

Kelsey looked at the three caring people in front of her and thought about how far she'd come. A year ago, she had been a frustrated employee with a dream of moving into management. Now she had earned her business degree and had taken her first steps with a great company.

She smiled with a sense of accomplishment, knowing her career was well on its way.

Legendary
Service
Self-Assessment
for Service
Providers

As a customer-facing service provider, you may find it helpful to take this self-assessment at about the same time you read this book. As you put what you have learned into practice and become more proficient in the five elements of the ICARE model, we suggest you occasionally reevaluate your development by rating yourself again. We think you'll be pleasantly surprised at how fast you can progress in all five areas once you become accustomed to focusing on service. Don't compare yourself to others or worry about reaching a perfect score of 100 points—concentrate on your own best score.

Rate yourself as follows on each of these statements.

1 = Never; 2 = Seldom; 3 = Fairly Often;
4 = Frequently; 5 = Always

Ideal Service

Your Score

1. I perform my tasks with my customer in mind. _____
2. I build lasting relationships with my customers. _____
3. I act on my belief that service is important. _____
4. I deliver Ideal Service on a daily basis. _____

Culture of Service

5. My daily interactions with customers demonstrate a willingness to serve. _____
6. I use the organization's vision and values to guide my decisions. _____
7. I provide memorable experiences that keep customers coming back. _____
8. My behaviors match my values. _____

Attentiveness

9. I profile my customers and their personal preferences. _____
10. I create positive first impressions with my customers. _____
11. I create positive last impressions with my customers. _____
12. I treat my internal customers as if they were paying customers. _____

	Your
## Responsiveness	Score

13. I ask clarifying questions to be sure I understand what my customer is saying. _____

14. I pay attention to my customer's nonverbal behaviors so that I can better understand his or her frame of mind. _____

15. I keep a positive attitude when dealing with difficult situations that involve my customers. _____

16. I demonstrate a willingness to serve my customers. _____

Empowerment

17. I share ideas for process improvement with my manager. _____

18. I look for ways to provide the "extra touch" for my customers. _____

19. I continue to increase my knowledge about my job. _____

20. I look for ways to perform my job better. _____

Total Score _____

Acknowledgments

Ken Blanchard

In reflecting on who I wanted to acknowledge in this book, I immediately thought of Sheldon Bowles, my coauthor on *Raving Fans*, and Barbara Glanz, my coauthor on *The Simple Truths of Service*. I learned so much about customer service from each of them.

Now I'm blessed with the opportunity to work with Kathy Cuff and Vicki Halsey. Kathy has been a key part of our company for 26 years. Her enthusiasm, passion for life, and inspiring way of teaching others are unmatched—except perhaps by Vicki Halsey, a woman who invented the phrase "high energy." Not only is Vicki a great teacher, but she is also one of the most creative developers of learning materials I've ever known. Working with Kathy and Vicki on this book is something I will never forget.

I want to thank my fabulous team on this project, led by Renee Broadwell and cheered on by Martha Lawrence. Margery Allen is my left and right hand who keeps me committed to my commitments. And when everyone's busy and something needs to be done, we have an excellent partner in Anna Espino.

Speaking of partners, I married way above myself. I can't praise my wife, Margie, enough for the impact she has had on my life and my work. Our kids, Scott and Debbie, aren't bad either! And I get to practice Legendary Service with my wonderful grandkids: Hannah, Atticus, Kurtis, Kyle, and the famous Alec. I'm a very lucky man.

Last but not least, I'd like to thank Alexandria Hamrick for inspiring our story.

Kathy Cuff

This book has been a work in progress for many years. My deepest appreciation to my colleagues and friends, Ken Blanchard and Vicki Halsey, who share a passion for customer service and agreed to write a book with me on this subject so that others can improve their relationships with their customers and, in turn, build their businesses. I also want to thank my husband, Ed, and my sons, Kevin and Brian, who encouraged me along the way to stick with my dream of writing this and seeing it through the rigorous process. Last but not least, I thank my mom, Gay Riley, who at 94 years old still teaches me daily, through her actions of showing others she cares about them, that each of us can make a difference in this world.

Vicki Halsey

The need for us to write this simple but powerful book has become increasingly obvious to us through the years. Organizations must create a space where people feel important and, consequently, where they can help their customers feel important. When customers and people in organizations collaborate to drive innovative practices, a synergy is produced that creates lasting relationships of care. I am especially grateful for my own lasting relationships of care, which have helped me clarify my beliefs and cowrite this book. My deepest gratitude goes to Ken Blanchard for his simple truths; to Kathy Cuff for her energy, drive, and wisdom; to Sarah Meeker and Nick Halsey for their initial editing and their focus on transformational ideas; to Renee Broadwell, our brilliant editor, for inspiring clarity and insight into the lives of customers; to Jake and Rick Halsey for their ever-present love; and to Elaine White, Pat Zigarmi, Margie Blanchard, and Debbie Blanchard for always encouraging me to grow, learn, and believe in myself. I also want to express my gratitude to my amazing clients, friends, and family who want me, above all, to express my truth and help create a world where people, in service to one another, can thrive.

About the Authors

Ken Blanchard

Few people have impacted the day-to-day management of people and companies more than Ken Blanchard. A prominent, gregarious, and sought-after author, speaker, and business consultant, Ken is universally characterized as one of the most insightful, powerful, and compassionate individuals in business today.

From his phenomenal bestselling book *The One Minute Manager* (coauthored with Spencer Johnson)—which has sold more than 15 million copies and has remained on bestseller lists for more than 30 years—to the library of 60 other books—among them *Leading at a Higher Level, Raving Fans, Gung Ho!,* and *Leadership and the One Minute Manager,* coauthored with outstanding practitioners—Ken's impact as a writer is extraordinary and far reaching. In July 2005, he was inducted into the amazon.com Hall of Fame as one of the top 25 bestselling authors of all time.

Ken is the chief spiritual officer of The Ken Blanchard Companies®, an international management training and consulting firm that he and his wife, Dr. Marjorie Blanchard, cofounded in 1979 in San Diego. Ken is also cofounder of Lead Like Jesus, a nonprofit organization focused on developing servant leaders in every sector of society. He is a trustee emeritus member of the board of trustees at his alma mater, Cornell University. The college of business at Grand Canyon University bears his name.

Ken and Margie have been married 51 years and live in San Diego. Their son, Scott, their daughter, Debbie, and Scott's wife, Madeleine, all hold key positions at The Ken Blanchard Companies.

Kathleen Riley Cuff

Kathy Cuff is a senior consulting partner with The Ken Blanchard Companies. Since joining Blanchard® in September 1987, she has worn many hats in the organization, her first being that of Ken Blanchard's events manager—a time period in which, Kathy later realized, she was actually being mentored by Ken for a future position in leadership training and development. In her current role, she delivers training and consulting services to clients on topics such as leadership, self-leadership, teams, change, and her passion, customer service. Kathy successfully works with people at all levels of an organization, from entry-level employees through C-level executives. Her background in training and development with a wide variety of clients gives her the ability to flex her style as needed to enhance each client's learning experience. She has trained in a wide array of industries, including retail, pharmaceutical, medical, financial, technology, healthcare, and government.

Kathy is coauthor, with Vicki Halsey, of Blanchard's Legendary Service customer service training program and is also coauthor of Ken Blanchard's bestselling book *Leading at a Higher Level*. In addition, she has coauthored many Blanchard custom products for her clients. Kathy is a regular contributor to The Ken Blanchard Companies' *LeaderChat* blog, which reaches more than 20,000 readers each month. Her monthly posts explore service topics—both internally with peers and externally with customers—to identify best practices in customer service and servant leadership. Kathy holds a bachelor of arts degree in speech communications from San Diego State University and has completed numerous professional development courses.

E-mail: Kathy.cuff@kenblanchard.com

kenblanchard.com/Why-Blanchard/Meet-Our-Experts/Kathy-Cuff

Victoria Halsey, PhD

Vicki Halsey is vice president of applied learning at The Ken Blanchard Companies. Coauthor with Kathy Cuff of Blanchard's Legendary Service customer service program and also Blanchard's award-winning Situational Leadership® II, Vicki is sought out globally to inspire people to unleash their passion and skill and drive organizational success. She has designed and facilitated leadership and service initiatives at hundreds of Fortune 500 organizations such as Microsoft, Wells Fargo, Nike, Disney, Shell Oil, Toyota, and Procter & Gamble. With the same skill and finesse that made her a national champion platform diver, Vicki dives in quickly and deeply with her clients to identify and address their needs and visions. People leave Vicki's presentations with renewed conviction that they can utilize their own brilliance to tackle key personal and organizational issues. Whether the audience is 50 or 5,000, Vicki's energy, intellect, and passion motivate people to unleash their greatness. Vicki is the author of the bestseller *Brilliance by Design* and coauthor of bestsellers *The Hamster Revolution*, *The Hamster Revolution for Meetings*, and Ken Blanchard's *Leading at a Higher Level*. She and her husband, Rick, have two sons and live in Escondido, California.

E-mail: Vicki.halsey@kenblanchard.com

Vickihalsey.com

kenblanchard.com/Why-Blanchard/Meet-Our-Experts/Vicki-Halsey

Services Available— The Ken Blanchard Companies®

Legendary Service training sessions at The Ken Blanchard Companies address two very critical groups in organizations: we show Service Providers—frontline, customer-facing employees—how, independently, they can take the lead in providing better service to customers; and we show Service Champions—leaders and managers—how to not only provide the framework for creating a culture of service but also define their role in the implementation of service within the organization. The ICARE model is put into practice as we drill down into the five aspects of Legendary Service in a comprehensive and interactive way. Contact us today at http://www.kenblanchard.com/Solutions/Engagement-and-Cultural-Change/Legendary-Service to learn more about becoming a customer-driven organization—one that is known for its Legendary Service.

The Ken Blanchard Companies is a global leader in workplace learning, productivity, performance, and leadership effectiveness that is best known for its Situational Leadership® II (SLII®) program—the most widely taught leadership model in the world. Because of its ability to help people excel as self-leaders and leaders of others, SLII® is embraced by Fortune 500 companies as well as small to midsize businesses, governments, and educational and nonprofit organizations.

Blanchard programs, which are based on the evidence that people are the key to accomplishing strategic objectives and driving business results, develop excellence in leadership, teams, customer loyalty, change management, and performance improvement. The company's continual research points to best practices for workplace improvement, while its world-class trainers and coaches drive organizational and behavioral change at all levels and help people make the shift from learning to doing.

Leadership experts from The Ken Blanchard Companies are available for workshops and consulting as well as for keynote addresses on organizational development, workplace performance, and business trends. Visit kenblanchard.com to learn about workshops, coaching services, and leadership programs to help your organization create lasting behavior changes that have a measurable impact.

The Ken Blanchard Companies
World Headquarters
125 State Place
Escondido, CA 92029
U.S.A.
+1 760 489 5005
International@kenblanchard.com
www.kenblanchard.com

United Kingdom

The Ken Blanchard Companies UK
+44 (0) 1483 456300
uk@kenblanchard.com

Canada

The Ken Blanchard Companies Canada
+1 800 665 5023
Canada@kenblanchard.com

Singapore

The Ken Blanchard Companies Singapore
+65 67751030
Singapore@kenblanchard.com

For an updated list of all global partners of The Ken Blanchard Companies, including contact information, please go to http://www.kenblanchard.com/About-Us/Global-Locations.

Join Us Online

Visit Blanchard on YouTube. Watch thought leaders from The Ken Blanchard Companies in action. Link and subscribe to Ken Blanchard's YouTube channel and you'll receive updates as new videos are posted.

Join the Blanchard Fan Club on Facebook. Be part of our inner circle and link to Ken Blanchard on Facebook. Meet other fans of Ken and his books, access videos and photos, and get invited to special events.

Join Conversations with Ken Blanchard. Ken Blanchard's blog site, HowWeLead.org, was created to inspire positive change. It is a public service site devoted to leadership topics that connect us all, a social network where you will meet people who care deeply about responsible leadership, and a place where Ken would like to hear your opinion.

Ken's Twitter Updates. Receive timely messages and thoughts from Ken. Find out about events he's attending, articles he's reading, and what's on his mind @kenblanchard.

How 2 Lead App. The free How2Lead app allows you to stay up to date with the latest in leadership, corporate training, and management practices. Read Blanchard blogs, access videos, and receive updates on new thought leadership and research. Compatible with Android phones and devices, iPhone, iPod Touch, and iPad.